CW01390645

BUXTON BRANCHES

BIRTH RECORDS

LeeAnn Simmers Dickey

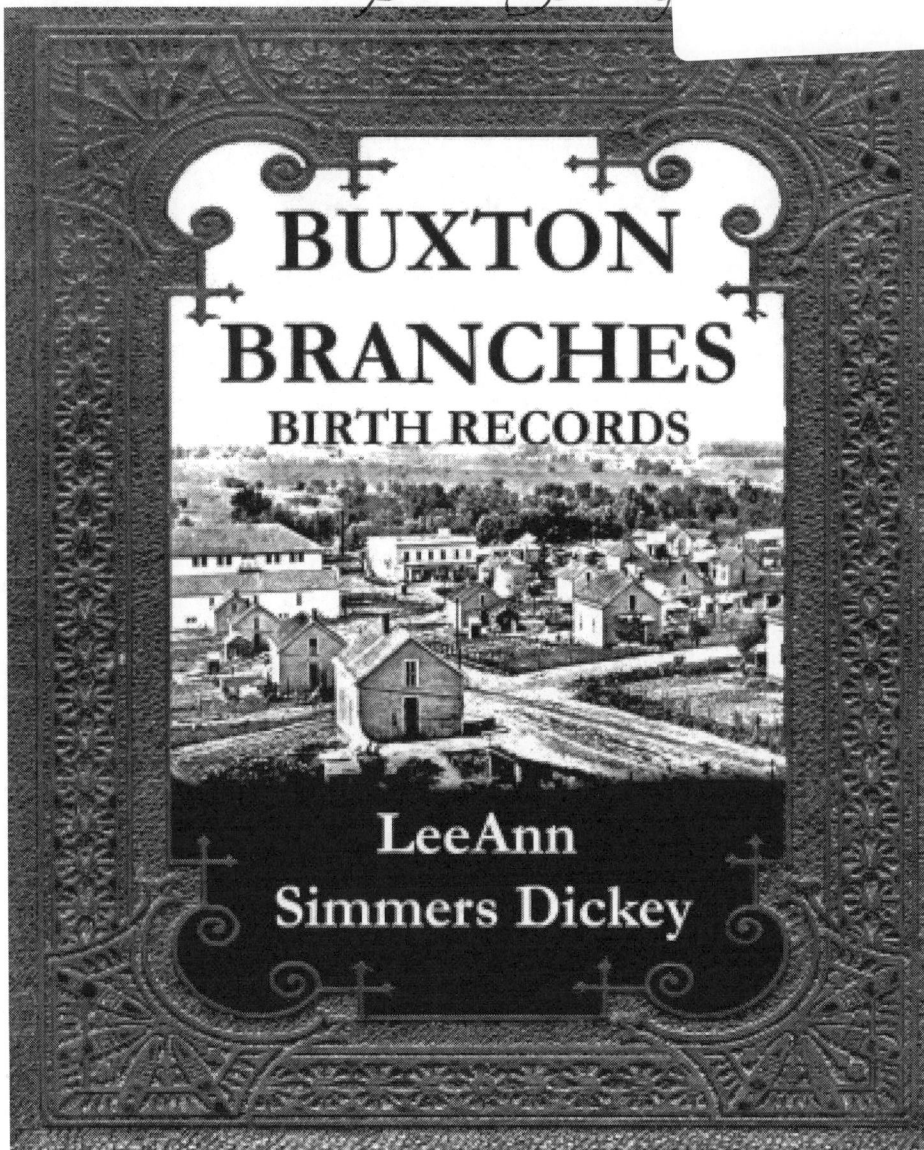

PBL Limited
Ottumwa, Iowa

Buxton Branches

Birth Records

Lee Ann Simmers Dickey

A view across Buxton. Note the many similar-styled houses.
There were about 2,000 such houses; each story-and-a-half structure contained five or
six rooms and each was sited on at least a quarter-acre.
The large two-story building in the center was the high school.

This book is dedicated to
all the families of Buxton --
the ones who lived there in harmony,
and the ones who remember

Lee Ann Simmers Dickey

Table of Contents

Author's Note

I would like to share a few comments on the birth records. Because names were often written down as they sounded, the spelling is incorrect on a lot of the official records. Names are recorded here as they appear in the record books at the Monroe County Courthouse.

How much information was collected and recorded about each birth and family varied greatly through the decades. All information which was included in the available records has been reproduced here.

Not all records are available to the researcher in the county where the birth took place. Some birth records were filed only at state level and not in the county. The two time periods when this occurred were July 1904 to July 1906, and July 1935 to June 1941. There may be a few births which were recorded in both places, and if the records were available to me, they are included here. For the most part, however, researchers have to go to state level to obtain birth records from those years.

At the time some of these records were created, "colored" was considered an appropriate descriptive term. I have therefore reproduced the records as they were recorded.

Records of stillbirths and illegitimate births are now closed to the public, making it difficult to trace these events. Without full access to the sealed records, it is impossible to determine how many stillbirths and illegitimate births actually occurred.

The county recorder's office does not do searches of the records, but makes the records available to researchers.

Before Buxton, Iowa came into existence, many of these families were living and mining an area in Mahaska County, Iowa called Muchakinock. Some members of Buxton families are buried in the Muchakinock cemetery. I hope my next project will include information which ties the Buxton families to their ancestors in Muchakinock, Iowa.

The railroad depot in Buxton.

I would like to thank my family first; they are the best. My thanks go also to the ladies at the courthouse who put up with me, and to my great support group of family and friends.

I hope these records will help those who are researching Buxton families. I wish good luck to all the researchers out there and their quests. Genealogy research is sometimes like walking back in time in someone else's life. At other times it is like hitting a brick wall. You may be the only one in your family to know all of the history, so write it down for future generations so they will know what the ancestors were like and where they came from.

I hope everyone enjoys the book and finds a lost relative or two. Thanks to everyone for all the help and support.

Lee Ann Simmers Dickey
Albia, Iowa
May, 2011

Buxton, Iowa -- An Integrated Mining Community

The community of Buxton, Iowa existed for little more than twenty years. Established in 1900 as a coal camp to house the workers who mined coal for the Consolidation Coal Company in southeastern Iowa, Buxton was located between the current-day towns of Oskaloosa and Albia. By 1910, the population was 5,000 – the largest unincorporated coal mining community in the state. It was also the largest community in Monroe County, with a population larger than the county seat.

Buxton was a model community where black and white citizens lived and worked side by side. In a state where 99 percent of the population at the time was white, the majority of Buxton's population (54 percent in 1905) was black.

Many of the black residents were coal miners and their families, imported from the South by Consolidation Coal Company which owned the surrounding coal mines. But Buxton also included black professionals (doctors, pharmacists, dentists, lawyers) and businessmen (farmers, landlords, shopkeepers, restaurateurs).

White and black residents were treated by black doctors; the company's chief surgeon was black. Black and white clerks manned the company store together. Black and white students shared classes, learning from teachers of both races. Interracial marriages were not only condoned but celebrated.

#15 Mine at Buxton, Iowa, with railroad cars ready to load with coal.

The people of Buxton, especially the black population, spoke of the town as Utopia – a place where they were free of the stifling restrictions of race. Ben Buxton, the superintendent of Consolidation Coal Company, would not tolerate anyone who treated blacks unfairly.

But though separations were not forced, blacks and whites held separate dances, attended separate churches, and belonged to separate lodges. Even though by today's standards it was not utopia, Buxton was unique for its time.

Towns like Buxton were called coal camps, built near the coal seams so miners could be easily transported to and from their work by special trains. Most coal camps were intended for use for no more than a decade. When local coal was exhausted, the camp would be moved to a location closer to new mines. Because of the short anticipated lifespan of the towns, sometimes little attention was paid to aesthetics or even to health concerns such as proper drainage.

In contrast, Buxton was a planned community with about 2,000 homes. Buxton was carefully laid out, sited on a rolling section of land which provided good drainage and air circulation. As a planned community, it included stores, churches, a YMCA, and schools, but (officially, at least) no taverns or saloons.

Each family home – there were about 2,000 in all – was a five- or six-room house sited on at least a quarter-acre of land, space which allowed gardening. Many families also raised chickens or kept a pig or cow. Each family had a cistern for water storage, with water delivered by the company. Five-room houses had a living room/parlor, dining room and kitchen downstairs, and two bedrooms upstairs. Six-room houses had an additional bedroom on the main floor. Each family had a coal shed and outhouse in the back yard.

The YMCA built by the company for its workers was said to be the largest in existence in the United States, with as many as 300 members. The three-story building, along with an annex intended for boys, included space for lodge meetings and an auditorium that would seat 1,000. Among the speakers hosted there was Booker T. Washington, who drew a more-than-capacity crowd.

There were four elementary schools and a high school. The school superintendent and high school principal were black, as were many teachers. While there was a whites-only private school, the public school system was fully integrated.

Though there was a company store operated by Consolidation Coal, residents and workers were not limited to shopping there. Other businesses were not only tolerated but encouraged. The company store, the Monroe Mercantile Company, was three full stories at first, but was rebuilt on a slightly-smaller scale after a devastating fire in 1910. The store boasted electric lights, electric elevators, and merchandise acquired by buyers who spent all their time in Chicago and New York.

Buxton had three newspapers, a bank, a millinery shop, a municipal band, women's clubs, fraternal lodges, and two baseball teams – one team was integrated, the other all black.

By 1920 production from the coal mines around Buxton had peaked and new mines were opened further away. Eventually the miners, too, moved on. Some followed Consolidation's mining operations to Haydock, Consol, and Bucknell. Some of Buxton's buildings were moved to those towns as well. Others were sold and moved by their new owners.

The town site of Buxton is listed on the National Register of Historic Places; it was entered on October 15, 1966.

From the Buxton Archives

May 1903 Tornado at Buxton
A tornado hit Buxton with lives lost: Georgia Blakley, Herbert Rhodes, Molellus Rhodes, and Eliza Blakely. The injured were Amphy and Minnie Blakely; Sewd, Lucy, Georg and Addison Rhodes; Buddie Reasby, and Mary Walker.

May 12, 1909
Buxton Laundry and Bakery Company destroyed by arson. $500.00 reward.

February 1911
Fire destroyed the Big Company Store.

October 1916
Cooperstown (an outlying section of Buxton) destroyed by fire: grocery store, new hotel property, two drug stores, cigar store, Masonic Hall, dance hall, billiard and pool hall.

Churches in Buxton included St. John's African Methodist Episcopal (A.M.E.), Mt. Zion Baptist. There was also a Mission A.M.E. Church for a while.

Social, Literary and Religious Clubs included Household of Ruth, Sunday School Union, Self Culture Club, Tabernacle Mission, White Vest Knights, Booker Washington Literary Society, Athenian Literary Society and Home and Foreign Mission Circle. The Etude Music Club was discussing the life of Beethoven. The Oreole Music Club was discussing the life of Mozart.

Fraternal Organizations included Masons, Odd Fellows, Elks, Knights of Pythias, Knights of Tabor and the Modern Woodsmen.

The Palimpsest of June 1945, in an article titled *The Rise and Fall of Buxton* said that the only colored registered woman pharmacist in Iowa was Mrs. Hattie Hutchinson. She

Two unidentified miners pulling away from one of the Buxton mines.

and her husband Ike owned a drug store to the south of town, an area known as "Sharp End."

Doctors included: Dr. E.A. Carter, Dr. C.G. Robinson, Dr. J.H. William, Dr. H.H. London, Dr. C.S. Taylor, Dr. J.R. Cross, Dr. H.B. Woods, Dr. James Muir, Dr. Traister, and Dr. Ralph O. Early.

Funeral Home Directors: S.C. Welch, H.C. Cunningham.

Lawyers: Geo. W. Woodson, Jas. Spears.

Undertaker: S. Billings.

Postmaster: Ed Mills.

Dentist: L.R. Willis.

Midwives: Old Lady Julia Ross, Mrs. Lucy Mealy, Mary E. Mash, Nellie Watson, Hattie Peterson, Mary Chambers, Mrs. Trenchak.

Music Teachers: Cora Thomas, Josie Meadows, Mollie Tibbs, Mrs. Will Lee, Mrs. DuMond.

Justice of the Peace: E.A. London.

Constables: Tom Romans.

Pharmacists: Mattie Hutchison, J. W. Neely.

Manie Lobbins had a livery barn at "Sharp End."

Rising Sun Restaurant was operated by Mrs. Anna Lobbins in Cooperstown.

Peter Carey's barber shop was also in Cooperstown across from Cooper's Store.

Madam Ella Yancy did hair dressing, face massage and chiropody. She was an honor graduate of New York College of Hairdressing.

Anderson Perkin and Son operated a hotel and confectionary near the depot.

Jeffers Restaurant was run by Andy and Maggie Jeffers.

Peter Abington, the caterer, kept his wagon on the street and sold ice cream, pies, bread, butter and eggs.

Lewis Reasby had a hamburger stand in front of the Y.M.C.A.

The Buxton Negro Concert Band was famous throughout southern Iowa and was led by F.E. Goggins.

The Langois sisters displayed motion pictures every night on the second floor of the Y.M.C.A. building. They were known as the "French Women."

Company Store operated by W.A. Wells.

Company Meat Market owned by Hobe Armstrong.

James Robert manufactured Cuban Handmade Havana Cigars.

Granberry Bros. manufactured tailor made clothes.

London & London, owned by E.A. London and W.H. London dealt in sewing machines and musical instruments and was located in the Thomas Block.

The Buxton *Advocate* newspaper, published weekly, was owned and operated by R.B. Montgomery.

Four unidentified Buxton residents show off the results after butchering hogs.

A little west of "Sharp End" was a grocery owned by J.W. Neely, who was also a pharmacist.

A.G. Rhodes had a shoe shop.

Rev. Lucas operated the bakery.

School Superintendent was Prof. Gilliam.

Schools: Fifth Street School, Eleventh Street School, Swede Town School. The High School was erected east of the Fifth Street School.

Buxton Birth Records (Book 1):
October 27, 1904 - October 1, 1905 Monroe County, Iowa

Information Recorded:

Full Name of Child, Sex, No. of Children to this Mother, Color (White, Black or Red), Hour of Birth, Date of Birth, Place of Birth, Born in Wedlock (yes or no), Father's Place of Birth, Father's Age, Mother's Place of Birth, Mother's Age, Mother's Maiden Name, Mother's Residence, Full Name of Father, Occupation, Name and Address of Medical or other Attendant.

Names may not be spelled correctly, because they are copied as they are written in the original records. These records are recorded at the state level but not at county level.

No.1 — **James Francis Schooley,** Male, 4, White, 8 p.m., October 27, 1904, Bluff Creek Twp., Yes, Monroe Co., Iowa, 40, Washington Co., Iowa, 36, Jennett Lyall Carrick, Bluff Creek Twp., Martin Luther Schooley, Farmer, Dr. S.T. Gray, Albia, Iowa

No. 2 — Missing

No.3 — **Frank Cowden**, Male, 5, White, 4 p.m., November 23, 1904, Buxton, Iowa, Yes, Eddyville, Iowa, 33, Farmington, Iowa, 29, Millie Brabhuin, Buxton, Iowa, William Cowden, Miner, Dr. H.B. Woods, Buxton, Iowa

No. 4 — **Edward Howard Odem**, Male, 5, White, 4 p.m., November 25, 1904, Buxton, Iowa, Yes, Eddyville, Iowa, 27, Tallmadge, Michigan, 25, May Bowman, Buxton, Iowa, Edward Odem, Day Labor, Dr. H.B. Woods, Buxton, Iowa

No. 5 — **Stillbirth Child,** Female, 3, Black, 6 a.m., December 7, 1904, Buxton, Iowa, Yes, Bragehill, Indiana, 24, Bergenham, Alabama, 22, Lallie Bradford, Buxton, Iowa, G.W. White, Miner, Dr. H.B. Woods, Buxton, Iowa

No.6 — **Richard Hockings**, Male, 3, White, 5:30 p.m., November 27, 1904, Buxton, Iowa Yes, England, 24, Streeter, Illinois, 24, Euphima Wier, Buxton, Iowa, Francis Hockings, Miner, Dr. H.B. Woods, Buxton, Iowa

No. 7 — **Orville Masters**, Male, 6, White, 7:30 p.m., October 20, 1904, Buxton, Iowa, Yes, Gainesville, Illinois, 42, Not Known, 28, Ida Colby, Buxton, Iowa, Albert Ross Masters, Miner, Dr. James Muir, Buxton, Iowa

No. 8 — **Anna Sears**, Female, 5, Black, 9:30 a.m., December 7, 1904, Buxton, Iowa, Yes, Cumberland Co., Virginia, 40, Moorland, West Virginia, 29, Eleza Jane Warren, Buxton, Iowa, Jesse M. Sears, Miner, Dr. H.B. Woods, Buxton, Iowa

No. 9 — **Milvin Iona Frazen**, Female, 1, White, 8 a.m., November 21, 1904, Buxton, Iowa, Yes, Kansas, 37, Eddyville, Not given, Maggie McCannon, Buxton, Iowa, John Frazen, Labor, Dr. H.B. Woods, Buxton, Iowa

No. 10 — **Wilbin McFall,** Male, 2, White, 6 a.m., December 17, 1904, Bluff Creek Twp., Yes, Oskaloosa, Iowa, 28, Marion County, Illinois, 24, Minney Long, Bluff Creek Twp., Fred McFall, Farmer, Dr. Otis Cobb, Lovilia, Iowa

No. 11 — **Virginia Pierson**, Female, 1, White, 2 a.m., December 15, 1904, Bluff Creek Twp., Yes, Sweden, 33, Mahaska, Colorado, 30, Agnes Spencer, Bluff Creek Twp., Fred Pierson, Miner, Dr. Otis Cobb, Lovilia, Iowa

No. 12 — **Unnamed Taylor**, Female, 9, White, 11:50 p.m., November 12, 1904, Bluff Creek Twp., Yes, Illinois, 40, Missouri, 38, Amy Taylor, Bluff Creek Twp., Elliott Taylor, Farmer, Dr. C.B. Powell, Albia, Iowa

No. 13 — **Roma Anderson,** Female, 4, Black, 11:45 a.m., January 1, 1905, Buxton, Iowa, Yes, Keokuk, Iowa, 38, St. Louis, Missouri, 27, Lulu Chatman, Buxton, Iowa, W. T. Anderson, Miner, Dr. H.B. Woods, Buxton, Iowa

No. 14 — **Gladys Mautel Lafayette**, Female, 3, Black, 2:30 a.m., December 26, 1905, Buxton, Iowa, Yes, Oskaloosa, Iowa, 31, Oskaloosa, Iowa, 25, Chrestina Gaut, Buxton, Iowa, Jesse Lafayette, Miner, Dr. James Muir, Buxton, Iowa

No. 15 — **Wilbert Campbell**, Male, 10, White, 4 p.m., December 7, 1905, Buxton, Iowa, Yes, England, 43, Monroe Co., Iowa, 42, Margaret Agness McCarty, Buxton, Iowa, James Joseph Campbell, Miner, Dr. James Muir, Buxton, Iowa

No. 16 — **Helen Weaver**, Female, 2, Black, 8 p.m., December 12, 1905, Buxton, Iowa, Yes, Pennsylvania, 29, St. John, Illinois, 22, Clara Getter, Buxton, Iowa, Lewis Weaver, Miner, Dr. H.B. Woods, Buxton, Iowa

No. 17 — **Ruby Estella May Gaines,** Female, 1, Black, 5 p.m., January 3, 1905, Buxton, Iowa, No, Not Given, 25, Not Given, 19, Myrtle Gaines, Buxton, Iowa, Frank Davis, Miner, Mrs. Lucy Mealy, midwife, Buxton, Iowa

No. 18 — **Stella Margaret Chapman**, Female, 5, Black, 10:15 a.m., January 9, 1905, Buxton, Iowa, Yes, Virginia, 39, Virginia 33, Millie James, Buxton, Iowa, John Chapman, Miner, Mrs. Lucy Mealy, midwife, Buxton, Iowa

No. 19 — **Harold Steney**, Male, 2, White, 4:30 p.m., January 9, 1905, Buxton, Iowa, Yes, Knoxville, Iowa, 24, Guthrie Co., Iowa, 24, Maude Jane Pettit, Des Moines, Iowa, Claude Leroy Steney, Miner, Mary E. Mash, midwife, Buxton, Iowa

No. 20 — **Raymond Nevins**, Male 7, White, 9:35 p.m., January 17, 1905, Buxton, Iowa, Yes, Buxton, Iowa, 33, Eddyville, Iowa, 32, Lulu Johnson, Buxton, Iowa, Charley Nevins, Teamster, Dr. H.B. Woods, Buxton, Iowa

No. 21 — **Charles H. Johnson**, Male, 3, Black, 12 a.m., January 11, 1905, Buxton, Iowa, Yes, Harrisburg, Pennsylvania, 25, Sparrows Point, Maryland, 22, Hattie Holland, Buxton, Iowa, Wm. E. Johnson, Miner, Mrs. Lucy Mealy, midwife, Buxton, Iowa

No. 22 — **Wm. E. Johnson**, Male 4, Black, 12:10 a.m., January 11, 1905, Buxton, Iowa, Yes, Harrisburg, Pennsylvania, 25, Sparrows Point, Maryland, 22, Hattie Holland, Buxton, Iowa, Wm. E. Johnson, Miner, Lucy Mealy, midwife, Buxton, Iowa

No. 23 — **John Willis Bradley**, Male 5, Black, 5 p.m., January 11, 1905, Buxton, Iowa, Yes, Charlottesville, Virginia, 45, Charlottesville, Virginia, 38, Ella Fry, Buxton, Iowa, Tandy Bradley, Miner, Mrs. Lucy Mealy, midwife, Buxton, Iowa

No. 24 — **Myrtle May Forgy**, Female, 3, Black, 9 a.m., January 19, 1905, Bluff Creek Twp., Yes, Virginia, 27, Illinois, 22, Daisy Watson, Bluff Creek Twp., Fred Forgy, Miner, Dr. Otis Cobb, Lovilia, Iowa

No. 25 — **Mangel Queen Taylor**, Female, 1, Black, 1:10 a.m., February 6, 1905, Buxton, Iowa, Yes, Higbee, Missouri, 25, Muchakinock, Iowa, 21, Selena Yancy, Buxton, Iowa, Warren W. Taylor, Coal Miner, Mrs. Lucy Mealy, midwife, Buxton, Iowa

No. 26 — **Lessie May Brown**, Female, 4, Black, 8:15 p.m., February 12, 1905, Buxton, Iowa, Yes, Stanton, Virginia, 25, Stanton, Virginia, 23, Lena Carey, Buxton, Iowa, French Brown, Coal Miner, Mrs. Lucy Mealy, Buxton, Iowa

No. 27 — **Margaret Ann Minarsick**, Female, 3, White, 5:35 p.m., February 13, 1905, Buxton, Iowa, Yes, Hungary, 26, Hungary, 21, Annie Subnar, Buxton, Iowa, George Minarsick, Coal Miner, Mrs. Lucy Mealy, Buxton, Iowa

No. 28 — **Alice Henrietta Wadlington**, Female, 7, Colored, 8 a.m., February 15, 1905, Buxton, Iowa, Yes, Rockingham, North Carolina, 33, Rockingham, North Carolina, 37, Addie Boyd, Buxton, Iowa, Henry Wadlington, Coal Miner, Mrs. Lucy Mealy, Buxton, Iowa

No. 29 — **Corarean Elizabeth Craggart**, Female, 4, Colored, 5:25 p.m., February 26, 1905, Buxton, Iowa, Yes, Virginia, 33, Virginia, 23, Mollie Elizabeth Wright, Buxton, Iowa, James Patterson Craggart, Miner, Mattie Watson, midwife, Buxton, Iowa

No. 30 — **Maurice Theodore Strang**, Male, 3, Colored, 9 a.m., February 26, 1905, Buxton, Iowa, Yes, Charlotte, Tennessee, 32, Clarksville, Tennessee, 32, Nannie Hutchison, Buxton, Iowa, Elmer Elsworth Strang, Delivery Man, Mrs. Lucy Mealy, midwife, Buxton, Iowa

No. 31 — **Lucy Marie Griffin**, Female, 1, White, 11 p.m., February 26, 905, Buxton, Iowa, Yes, Monroe Co., Iowa, 21, Muchakinock, Iowa, 18, Annie Vaughn, Buxton, Iowa, Not Given, Laborer, Dr. James Muir, Buxton, Iowa

No. 32 — **LuElla Rifle,** Female, 2, Colored, 5 p.m., February 28, 1905, Buxton, Iowa, Yes, Memphis, Tennessee, 28, Chariton, Iowa, 18, Edna May Marlow, Buxton, Iowa, George Rifle, Miner, Mrs. Lucy Mealy, Buxton, Iowa

No. 33 — **Robert Wesley Massey**, Male, 3, Colored, 11 p.m., March 1, 1905, Buxton, Iowa, Yes, Virginia, 39, California, Missouri, 21, Zephia Gertrude Jones, Buxton, Iowa, Mick Massey, Coal Miner, Mrs. Lucy Mealy, midwife, Buxton, Iowa

No. 34 — **Harold Sylvester Neal**, Male, 1, Colored, 6:45 a.m., March 3, 1905, Buxton, Iowa, Yes, Springfield, Illinois, 24, Charlottesville, Virginia, 21, Mobelia Snead, Buxton, Iowa, Geo. R. Neal, Coal Miner, Mrs. Lucy Mealy, midwife, Buxton, Iowa

Buxton Branches

No. 35 — **Mary Susan Milton**, Female, 14, Colored, 7:30 a.m., March 4, 1905, Buxton, Iowa, Yes, Georgia, 33, Marion Co., Alabama, 31, Susan Lumption, Buxton, Iowa, Frank Milton, Miner, Mary E. Mash, midwife, Buxton, Iowa

No. 36 — **Guy Hamlin Crauk**, Male, 8, Colored, 3:50 a.m., March 10, 1905, Buxton, Iowa, Yes, Charlottesville, Virginia, 44, Stanton, Virginia, 35, Mary Susan Harris, Buxton, Iowa, Benett Taylor Crauk, Miner, Dr. James Muir, Buxton, Iowa

No. 37 — **Orville Williams**, Male, 7, Colored, 6:20 a.m., March 10, 1905, Buxton, Iowa, Yes, Huntsville, Alabama, 44, Pine Bluff, Arkansas, 30, Louisa Mason, Buxton, Iowa, George Williams, Miner, Mrs. Lucy Mealy, midwife, Buxton, Iowa

No. 38 — **Henry Jackson**, Male, 2, Colored, 1:15 p.m., March 12, 1905, Buxton, Iowa, Yes, Ohio, 34, Iowa, 21, Mary Burger, Buxton, Iowa, Henry Jackson, Miner, Dr. H.B. Woods, Buxton, Iowa

No. 39 — **Vivian Slina Portugal**, Female, 4, White, 4:15 p.m., March 15, 1905, Buxton, Iowa, Yes, Essen, Germany, 35, Oskaloosa, Iowa, 34, Ora M. Wilcox, Buxton, Iowa, Chas. P. Portugal, Mine Worker, Dr. James Muir, Buxton, Iowa

No. 40 — **Jno. Robert Johnson**, Male, 1, Colored, 6 p.m., March 19, 1905, Buxton, Yes, Excelsior, Iowa, 19, Muchakinok, Iowa, 19, Elnora Toliver, Buxton, Iowa, Albert Johnson, Coal Miner, Mrs. Lucy Mealy, midwife, Buxton, Iowa

No. 41 — **Bertie Roberson,** Male, 1, Colored, 3 a.m., March 27, 1905, Buxton, Iowa, Yes, Howard Co., Missouri, 39, Nashville, Tennessee, 32, Ella Williams, Buxton, Iowa, William Alfred Roberson, Laborer, Dr. James Muir, Buxton, Iowa

No. 42 — **Bertha Sesh**, Female, 2, White, 5 a.m., March 28, 1905, Buxton, Iowa, Yes, Pennsylvania, 30, Iowa, 20, Cora Shuey, Buxton, Iowa, William Sesh, Miner, Dr. H.B. Woods, Buxton, Iowa

No. 43 — **Fern McKerson**, Female, 4, Colored, 8:30 —, March 28, 1905, Buxton, Iowa, Yes, Kansas, 32, Kansas, 19, Wistilda Brown, Buxton, Iowa, Jake McKerson, Miner, Mrs. Mary E. Mash, midwife, Buxton, Iowa

No. 44 — **Clarence Edward Minard**, Male, 1, White, 8:45 a.m., March 29, 1905, Buxton, Iowa, Yes, Iowa, 23, Indiana, 23, Zelda S. Rogers, Buxton, Iowa, John ? Minard, Laborer, Dr. H.B. Woods, Buxton, Iowa

One of the smaller Buxton houses. This photo is dated 1913.

No. 45 — **Arthur Sanery Montier**, Male, 1, Colored, 6 p.m., March 28, 1905, Buxton, Iowa, No, Not Given, Not Given, Cleveland, Iowa, 18, Ruth Colees, Buxton, Iowa, Arthur Montier, Cook, Mrs. Lucy Mealy, Buxton, Iowa

No. 46 — **Hannah Kline**, Female, 2, White, 10 p.m., April 2, 1905, Bluff Creek Twp., Yes, Iowa, 38, Iowa, 25, Mary McMurray, Bluff Creek Twp., Hall Kline, Farmer, Otis Cobb, Lovilia, Iowa

No. 47 — **James Garnett, Jr.**, Male, 1, Colored, 11 p.m., April 4, 1905, Buxton, Iowa, Yes, Virginia, 23, Iowa, 18, Virgia See Carson, Buxton, Iowa, James Garnett, Miner, Mrs. Lucy Mealy, Buxton, Iowa

No. 48 — **Benjamin Sirak/Sirvak**, Male, 3, White, 2 a.m., April 4, 1905, Buxton, Iowa, Yes, Hungary, 33, Hungary, 27, Mary Demock, Buxton, Iowa, Charles Sirak/Sivak, Miner, Mrs. Lucy Mealy, Buxton, Iowa

No. 49 — **Ollie Rhodes**, Male, 2, Colored, 11:30 a.m., April 5, 1905, Buxton, Iowa, Yes, Virginia, 26, Virginia, 24, Mary Ragsdale, Buxton, Iowa, W.B. Rhodes, Miner, Nellie Watson, Buxton, Iowa

No. 50 — **Evangline Larine Johnson**, Female, 5, White, 3:30 p.m., April 7, 1905, Buxton, Iowa, Yes, Iowa, 38, Iowa, 24, Lucy C. Coglesong, Buxton, Iowa, G.D. Johnson, Miner, Dr. H.B. Woods, Buxton, Iowa

No. 51 — **Charles Albert Davis**, Male, 2, Colored, 8 a.m., April 5, 1905, Buxton, Yes, Lebenon, Illinois, 30, Muchakinock, Iowa, 23, Sarah Frances Downey, Buxton, Iowa, Charles Edward Davis, Miner, Mrs. Lucy Mealy, midwife, Buxton, Iowa

No. 52 — **Prince Edward Miller**, Male, 1, Colored, 2:30 p.m., April 8, 1905, Buxton, Iowa, Yes, Bibb Co. Alabama, 26, Shelby Co. Alabama, 19, Luddie Mondeth, Buxton, Iowa, Prince Miller, Miner, Mrs. Lucy Mealy, midwife, Buxton, Iowa

No. 53 — **Izma Ophelia Robinson,** Female, 3, Colored, 3:10 p.m., April 10, 1905, Buxton, Iowa, Yes, Nelson Co. Virginia, 36, Franklin Co. Virginia, 35, Mollie Cooper, Buxton, Iowa, Nelson Robinson, Miner, Lucy Mealy, midwife, Buxton, Iowa

No. 54 — **Malvern Everett Wesley**, Male, 8, Colored, 2:20 a.m., April 14, 1905, Buxton, Iowa, Yes, Newport, Virginia, 43, Cobhan, Virginia, 37, Sarah Mc Kinney, Buxton, Iowa, James W. Wesley, Miner, Dr. James Muir, Buxton, Iowa

No. 55 — **Ida Delores Carter,** Female, 10, Colored, 9:20 p.m., April 20, 1905, Buxton, Iowa, Yes, Alabama, 43, Alabama, 33, Sarah Tanzel, Buxton, Iowa, S.J. Carter, Miner, Nellie Wilson, Buxton, Iowa

No. 56 — **Unnamed Neil**, Female, 4, White, 11 a.m., April 20, 1905, Bluff Creek Twp., Yes, Monroe Co. Iowa, Not Given, Kansas, Not Given, Lucy Dannels, Bluff Creek Twp., Jesse Neil, Farmer, Dr. Burk Powell, Albia, Iowa

No. 57 — **Jessie Mason**, Male, 1, Colored, 7 a.m., April 27, 1905, Buxton, Iowa, Yes, Virginia, 31, Kentucky, 14, Lulu Frazier, Buxton, Iowa, J.W. Mason, Miner, Dr. H.B. Woods, Buxton, Iowa

No. 58 — **Unnamed Gray**, Female, 2, White, 3:30 p.m., March 24, 1905, Bluff Creek Twp., No, Monroe Co. Iowa, 37, Monroe Co. Iowa, 35, Mary Eva Gray, County Poor Farm, Sam Gray, Farmer, Dr. T.E. Gutch, Albia, Iowa

No. 59 — **Jesse Randolph Willis**, Male, 2, Colored, 5:40 a.m., April 21, 1905, Buxton, Iowa, Yes, Charlottesville, Virginia, 29, Muchakinock, Iowa, 22, Lula Ann Gibbons, Buxton, Iowa, George Emmitt Willis, Miner, Mrs. Lucy Mealy, midwife, Buxton, Iowa

No. 60 — **Ester May Stewart**, Female, 3, Colored, 7 a.m., April 23, 1905, Buxton, Iowa, Yes, Georgia, 47, South Carolina, 28, Betty Larkes, Buxton, Iowa, George Stewart, Miner, Mrs. Lucy Mealy, midwife, Buxton, Iowa

No. 61 — **Jenoba Ladelle Dozier**, Female, 2, Colored, 6:10 a.m., April 25, 1905, Buxton, Yes, Lumpkins, Georgia, 29, Randolph, Georgia, 25, Mamie Ethel Brown, Buxton, Iowa, Henry Dozier, Miner, Mrs. Lucy Mealy, midwife, Buxton, Iowa

No. 62 — **Thomas Williams**, Male, 1, Colored, 2:10 p.m., May 1, 1905, Buxton, Iowa, Yes, Missouri, 39, Virginia, 37, Betty Johnson, Buxton, Iowa, Thomas Williams, Miner, Mary E. Mash, midwife, Buxton, Iowa

No. 63 — **Ethel May Rose**, Female, 1, Colored, 2:30 a.m., May 4, 1905, Buxton, Iowa, Yes, Ohio, 26, Missouri, 21, Rosie Feniell, Buxton, Iowa, William M. Rose, Miner, Mary E. Mash, midwife, Buxton, Iowa

No. 64 — **Ople Floradin Langly**, Female, 3, Colored, 6:05 a.m., May 8, 1905, Buxton, Iowa, Yes, Kentucky, 29, Tennessee, 31, Mary Dunnill, Buxton, Iowa, John Langly, Miner, Mary E. Mash, midwife, Buxton, Iowa

No. 65 — **Anna Rebeccah Holland**, Female, 8, Colored, 3:25 p.m., May 9, 1905, Buxton, Yes, Virginia, 42, Virginia, 31, Lulu Muse, Buxton, Iowa, Wm. H. Holland, Miner, Mrs. Lucy Mealy, midwife, Buxton, Iowa

No. 66 — **Unnamed Furgeson**, Female, 8, White, 1:30 a.m., May 12, 1905, Bluff Creek Twp., Yes, Iowa, 43, Pennsylvania, 38, Jennie Lewis, Bluff Creek Twp., Adephit Furgeson, Farmer, H.W. Nye, Not Given

No. 67 — **George Willis Pentleton,** Male, 3, Colored, 9 p.m., May 18, 1905, Buxton, Iowa, Yes, Mississippi, 28, Alabama, 24, Ophelia Thomas, Buxton, Iowa, John Henry Pentleton, Miner, Mrs. Lucy Mealy, midwife, Buxton, Iowa

No. 68 — **Victor Hugo Booker**, Male, 2, Colored, 8:20 p.m., May 13, 1905, Buxton, Iowa, Yes, Virginia, 34, Virginia, 23, Sarah Gobb, Buxton, Iowa, R.A. Booker, Nellie Watson, Buxton, Iowa

No. 69 — **Gertie May Bringman**, Female, 3, White, 12:15 a.m., May 22, 1905, Buxton, Iowa, Yes, Iowa, 48, Iowa, 29, Lottie Bringman, Buxton, Warren D. Bringman, Plasterer, Dr. H.B. Woods, Buxton, Iowa

No. 70 — **Harvey Wayne Thomas**, Male, 2, White, 2:00 p.m., May 21, 1905, Buxton, Iowa, Yes, Muchakinock, Iowa, 28, Oskaloosa, Iowa, 22, Bessie E. Humphrey, Buxton, Harvey W. Thomas, Miner, Dr. James Muir, Buxton, Iowa

No. 71 — **Ralph Albert McBride,** Male, 1, White, 3:50 p.m., May 31, 1905, Buxton, Iowa, Yes, Ottumwa, Iowa, 24, Des Moines, Iowa, 20, Ethel Lee Childs, Buxton, Iowa, Thomas Edgar McBride, Laborer, Dr. James Muir, Buxton, Iowa

No. 72 — **Mary Ella Walker**, Female, 4, Colored, 11:30 a.m., June 9, 1905, Buxton, Iowa, Yes, Alabama, 32, Missouri, 23, Annie Rucker, Buxton, George Walker, Coal Miner, Mrs. Lucy Mealy, midwife, Buxton, Iowa

No. 73 — **Louise Cordella Turner**, Female, 6, Black, 10 p.m., June 14, 1905, Buxton, Iowa, Yes, Illinois, 31, Alabama, 34, Eunice Winfred Kinsly, Buxton, Iowa, Wm. Edward Turner, Miner, Mrs. Lucy Mealy, midwife, Buxton, Iowa

No. 74 — **Mildred Lona McDowell**, Female, 1, White, 11 a.m., June 14, 1905, Buxton, Iowa, Yes, Illinois, 25, Wales, 21, Margaret J. McDowell, Buxton, Iowa, Herbert Lee McDowell, Miner, Dr. H.B. Woods, Buxton, Iowa

No. 75 — **G. Henry Washington,** Male, 5, Colored, 7 p.m., June 17, 1905, Buxton, Iowa, Yes, Virginia, 30, Virginia, 25, Francis Stribbling, Buxton, William Washington, Miner, Dr. H.B. Woods, Buxton, Iowa

No. 76 — **Norman Webb,** Male, 1, Colored, 12:30 p.m., June 19, 1905, Buxton, Iowa, No, Iowa, 21, Missouri, 15, Ona Webb, Buxton, Iowa, Tug Wilson, Miner, Dr. H.B. Woods, Buxton, Iowa

No. 77 — **Bessie Carrick,** Female, 6, White, 10:45 p.m., May 31, 1905, Bluff Creek Twp., Yes, Monroe Co. Iowa, 30, Albany, Iowa, 25, Mamie Stagg, Bluff Creek Twp., Frank Carrick, Farmer, S.T. Gray, Albia, Iowa

No. 78 — **Ella Bell Sharp,** Female, 1, Colored, 1:50 a.m., May 31, 1905, Buxton, Iowa, Yes, Kentucky, 29, Kentucky, 25, Lucy Black, Buxton, William Sharp, miner, Dr. H.B. Woods, Buxton, Iowa

No. 79 — **Clotia Willard Sharp,** Female, 2, Colored, 2:10 a.m., May 31, 1905, Buxton, Iowa, Yes, Kentucky, 29, Kentucky, 25, Lucy Black, Buxton, Iowa, William Sharp, Miner, Dr. H.B. Woods, Buxton, Iowa

No. 80 — **Unnamed Moore,** Male, 3, White, 2 p.m., June 3, 1905, Bluff Creek Twp., Yes, Monroe Co. Iowa, 36, Ireland, 34, Lizzie Falon, Bluff Creek Twp., Wm. Moore, Farmer, S.T. Gray, Albia, Iowa

No. 81 — **Gladys Ester Glen,** Female, 3, White, 3 a.m., June 4, 1905, Buxton, Iowa, Yes, Iowa, 37, Iowa, 35, Loie Ruggles, Buxton, Iowa, James Glenn, Teamster, Dr. H.B. Woods, Buxton, Iowa

No. 82 — **June Eve Calvert,** Female, 1, White, 3 a.m., June 5, 1905, Buxton, Iowa, Yes, Illinois, 22, Illinois, 18, Goldie Houstan, Buxton, Iowa, Harry Calvert, Teamster, Dr. H.B. Woods, Buxton, Iowa

No. 83 — **James William Trophy,** Male, 4, Colored, 5:25 p.m., June 16, 1905, Buxton, Iowa, Yes, Virginia, 35, Virginia, 22, Annie Mains, Buxton, Iowa, Allen Trophy, Miner, Mrs. Lucy Mealy, midwife, Buxton, Iowa

No. 84 — **Theodore Joseph Jackson**, Male, 3, Colored, 10:30 a.m., June 20, 1905, Buxton, Iowa, Yes, Virginia, 45, Virginia, 33, Elzzee Harris, Buxton, Iowa, Geo. W. Jackson, Miner, Mrs. Lucy Mealy, midwife, Buxton, Iowa

Looking east on 1st Street, Buxton. The large building to the right is the YMCA; the company store is visible on the left side of the street in the distance.

No. 85 — **Daniel M. Smith,** Male, 5, Colored, 9 p.m., June 22, 1905, Buxton, Iowa, Yes, Virginia, 31, Virginia, 27, Amy L. Martin, Buxton, Iowa, Daniel M. Smith, Miner, Mrs. Lucy Mealy, midwife, Buxton, Iowa

No. 86 — **Unnamed Scribner,** Female, 2, White, 3:30 a.m., July 2, 1905, Bluff Creek Twp., Yes, Monroe Co. Iowa, 27, Monroe Co. Iowa, 21, Lyda Debra Neil, Bluff Creek Twp., Geo. Scribner, Farmer, Dr. F. M. McCrea, Eddyville, Iowa

No. 87 — **Sallie May Arthur**, Female, 10, Colored, 9:40 a.m., July 2, 1905, Buxton, Iowa, Yes, Virginia, 39, Virginia, 34, Sallie May Tauks, Buxton, Iowa, Geo. Arthur, Miner, Mrs. Lucy Mealy, midwife, Buxton, Iowa

No. 88 — **Eva Mattie McDonald,** Female, 6, Colored, 9 a.m., July 3, 1905, Buxton, Iowa, Yes, Alabama, 53, Tennessee, 30, Fannie Murphy, Buxton, Jim McDonald, Miner, Dr. H.B. Woods, Buxton, Iowa

No. 89 — **Unnamed Harper,** Male, 2, White, Not Given, June 5, 1905, Bluff Creek Twp., Yes, Albia, Iowa, Not Given, Albia, Iowa, Not Given, Jessie Harper, Bluff Creek Twp., Jesse Harper, Farmer, Dr. C.B. Powell, Albia, Iowa

No. 90 — **Unnamed Carhart,** Female, 2, White, Not Given, June 13, 1905, Bluff Creek Twp., Yes, Albia, Iowa, Not Given, Albia, Iowa, Not Given, May DeTar, Bluff Creek Twp., John Carhart, Farmer, Dr. C.B. Powell, Albia, Iowa

No. 91 — **Louis Theophilus Ampy**, Male, 9, Colored, 10 a.m., June 18, 1905, Buxton, Iowa, Yes, Virginia, 63, Virginia, 39, Lue Harris, Buxton, Iowa, John Ampy, Miner, Mrs. Lucy Mealy, midwife, Buxton, Iowa

No. 92 — **Frank Tedro**, Male, 7, White, 6 a.m., June 19, 1905, Buxton, Iowa, Yes, Austria, 46, Austria, 38, Mary Maslay, Buxton, Iowa, John Tedro, Farmer, Mrs. Lucy Mealy, midwife, Buxton, Iowa

No. 93 — **Lula May Brooks,** Female, 4, Colored, 2 p.m., June 25, 1905, Buxton, Iowa, Yes, Virginia, 35, Tennessee, 24, Lula Rollan, Buxton, Iowa, Geo. W. Brooks, Miner, Mrs. Lucy Mealy, midwife, Buxton, Iowa

No. 94 — **Cossins Beaman,** Male, 2, Colored, 10 p.m., June 27, 1905, Buxton, Iowa, Yes, Alabama, 37, Missouri, 24, Julia Boyd, Buxton, Iowa, Archie Beaman, Miner, Mrs. Lucy Mealy, midwife, Buxton, Iowa

No. 95 — **Unnamed Michael,** Male, 7, Colored, 10 p.m., July 13, 1905, Buxton, Iowa, Yes, North Carolina, 37, North Carolina, 31, Delia, Weston, Buxton, Iowa, William Michael, Miner, H.G. Young, Buxton, Iowa

No. 96 — **Mabel Fullerton,** Female, 3, White, 5 p.m., July 14, 1905, Bluff Creek Twp., Yes, Bluff Creek Twp., 32, Bluff Creek Twp., 26, Mina A. Mahin, Bluff Creek Twp., Guy T. Fullerton, Farmer, S.T. Gray, Albia, Iowa

No. 97 — **Benjamin Roy Stanton,** Male, 1, Colored, 4 a.m., August 2, 1905, Buxton, Iowa, No, Missouri, 21, Rendville, Ohio ?, 22, Hattie Parker, Buxton, Iowa, Lee Stanton, Coal Mining, Mrs. Lucy Mealy, midwife, Buxton, Iowa

No. 98 — **Unnamed Calbert,** Male, 1, White, 11:15 a.m., August 13, 1905, Buxton, Iowa, Yes, Illinois, 22, Iowa, 21, Delta Bath, Buxton, Iowa, Robert Calbert, Miner, Dr. H.B. Woods, Buxton, Iowa

No. 99 — **James Arthur Jacobs,** Male, 3, Colored, 9 p.m., August 15, 1905, Buxton, Iowa, Yes, Marshall, Missouri, 29, Roanoke, Missouri, 26, Annie Gauary, Buxton, Iowa, James Jacobs, Coal Mining, Mrs. Lucy Mealy, midwife, Buxton, Iowa

No. 100 — **Claudine Leta Ross,** Female, 1, White, 11:20 a.m. September 2, 1905, Buxton, Iowa, Yes, Lucas Co. Iowa, 26, Pender, Nebraska, 18, Bertha Pierce, Buxton, Iowa, George C. Ross, Liveryman, Dr. James Muir, Buxton, Iowa

No. 101 — **Mary Watson,** Female, 9, White, 4:20 p.m., September 3, 1905, Buxton, Iowa, Yes, Scotland, 39, Scotland, 36, Maggie Ritchie, Buxton, Iowa, Jas. Watson, Miner, Dr. James Muir, Buxton, Iowa

No. 102 — **Walter Henry Reeves,** Male, 4, Colored, 8 p.m., September 4, 1905, Buxton, Iowa, Yes, Virginia, 28, Virginia, 25, Gertrude Carey, Buxton, Iowa, Walter Reeves, Miner, Mrs. Lucy Mealy, midwife, Buxton, Iowa

No. 103 — **Jesse Wilmiot Greaver,** Male, 2, Colored, 5:15 p.m., September 5, 1905, Buxton, Iowa, Yes, Virginia, 25, Virginia, 22, Cornelia Brown, Buxton, Iowa, Henry Greaver, Mining, Mrs. Lucy Mealy, midwife, Buxton, Iowa

No. 104 — **Thornton Briscoe Consart,** Male, 1, Black, 2:10 p.m., September 13, 1905, Buxton, Iowa, Yes, South Carolina, 33, Iowa, 22, Margaret M. Coleman, Buxton, Iowa, Shepherd Paris Consart, Miner, Mrs. Lucy Mealy, midwife, Buxton, Iowa

No. 105 — **Mary Robenson,** Female, 1, Colored, 6 a.m., July 29, 1905, Buxton, Iowa, Yes, Pennsylvania, 33, Tennessee, 19, Hattie Hale, Buxton, Iowa, Claude Robenson, Miner, Sealer Milton, Buxton, Iowa

No. 106 — **Fenerd Williams,** Male, 1, Colored, 12:30 p.m., October 21, 1905, Buxton, Iowa, Yes, Kentucky, 38, Alabama, 18, Beatrice Stiel, Buxton, Iowa, Chas. Williams, Miner, Dr. H.B. Woods, Buxton, Iowa

No. 107 — **Arthur Royal Hurly,** Male, 9, Colored, 9 a.m., September 21, 1905, Buxton, Iowa, Yes, Virginia, 32, Virginia, 28, Cora Moorman, Buxton, Iowa, James Hurly, Miner, Mrs. Lucy Mealy, midwife, Buxton, Iowa

No. 108 — **John Clay Wheels,** Male, 13, Colored, 2 p.m., October 1, 1905, Buxton, Iowa, Yes, Virginia, 50, Missouri, 41, Amanda Clay, Buxton, Iowa, James Wheels, Miner, Mrs. Lucy Mealy, midwife, Buxton, Iowa

Monroe County, Iowa Birth Book 2
1897-1908

Information recorded:
This county record book of births includes child's name, sex of child, date of birth, where child was born, father's name and mother's name. The page number of the record book where the birth is recorded has been included for the convenience of researchers.

PAGE 2:
Arthur, Cora Love Josephine — Female, April 25, 1902, Buxton, Iowa, Father: Thomas Arthur, Mother: Josephine Rosalie Carter

Anderson, Oscar William — Male, May 31, 1902, Buxton, Iowa, Father: Frank Edward Anderson, Mother: Iola Augusta Carlson

PAGE 3:
Anderson, Leslie Franklin — Male, March 7, 1907, Buxton, Iowa, Father: William Anderson, Mother: Lula Chapman

PAGE 4:
Antoe, Mary — Female, October 10, 1908, Buxton, Iowa, Father: George Antoe, Mother: Mary Copsard

Adams, Edna Beatrice — Female, February 20, 1908, Buxton, Iowa, Father: Bert Adams, Mother: Myrtle Claver

PAGE 20:
Brooks, Richard Bernard — Male, December 5, 1901, Buxton, Iowa, Father: Richard Brooks, Mother: Mary Ann Braslin

Bradley, Offie — Female, October 10, 1901, Buxton, Iowa, Father: Tansie Bradley, Mother: Ella Fry

PAGE 21:
Brock, Harold Wesley — Male, July 12, 1902, Buxton, Iowa, Father: Wesley H. Brock, Mother: Esther Janie Haycock

Brown, Felton Weslie — Male, September 25, 1902, Buxton, Iowa, Father: Jacob Franklin Brown, Mother: Hattie Louisa Williams

Blackman, Viola — Female, February 1, 1902, Buxton, Iowa, Father: Early Blackman, Mother: Rena Walker

Bryson, Izora — Female, February 7, 1902, Buxton, Iowa, Father: William Sherman Bryson, Mother: Maggie White

Benson, Algot Obert — Male, September 28, 1902, Buxton, Iowa, Father: Otto Benson, Mother: Hilda Christena Carlson

PAGE 23:
Buckler, Leota Fay — Female, July 31, 1904, Buxton, Iowa, Father: Siren Buckler, Mother: Martha Clara Ross

Booker, Irvin Anderson — Male, December 26, 1906, Buxton, Iowa. Father: Robert Anderson Booker, Mother: Sarah Gaff

Bradley, Henry Clay — Male, July 13, 1906, Buxton, Iowa, Father: Tandy B. Bradley, Mother: Tammy Ellen Fry

Bradley, Lillian Clear — Female, July 13, 1906, Buxton, Iowa, Father: Tandy B. Bradley, Mother: Tammy Ellen Fry

Brown, Not Named — Male, August 12, 1906, Buxton, Iowa, Father: French Brown, Mother: Lena Carey

Benson, Eva Elizabeth — Female, December 4, 1906, Buxton, Iowa, Father: Otto Benson, Mother: Matilda Anderson

PAGE 24:
Burgess, Buster Brown — Male, June 19, 1906, Buxton, Iowa, Father: Howard Burgess, Mother: Ellen Matilda Hunter

PAGE 26:

Buckingham, Rollin Scott — Male, July 22, 1908, Buxton, Iowa, Father: Rosco Dye Buckingham, Mother: Elizabeth Scott

Ball, Charles Manford — Male, May 22, 1908, Buxton, Iowa, Father: Arthur Lewis Ball, Mother: Minnie Lee Fish

Buttram, Boaz — Male, June 15, 1908, Buxton, Iowa, Father: Henry Buttram, Mother: Lucy Smith

Burkett, Ruth E. — Female, January 20, 1908, Buxton, Iowa, Father: Phillip Burkett, Mother: Mary E. Wheeler

Brooks, Geo. Alfred — Male, June 30, 1908, Buxton, Iowa, Father: Geo. Brooks, Mother: Lula Roland

PAGE 74:

Chapman, Hazel Dell — Female, July 10, 1902, Buxton, Iowa, Father: John Johnson Chapman, Mother: Willie Ann James

Courter, Margaret Aline — Female, June 9, 1902, Buxton, Iowa, Father: Miles Irving Courter, Mother: Edith M. Stockley

Carlson, Arthur Erenus — Male, July 5, 1902, Buxton, Iowa, Father: Carl Otto Carlson, Mother: Emma Louisa Carlson (No Maiden Name Given)

PAGE 75:

Crozier, Martin — Male, March 3, 1904, Buxton, Iowa, Father: George Crozier, Mother: Nora Hewit

PAGE 76:

Crawford, Carrie Viola — Female, September 22, 1906, Buxton, Iowa, Father: Silas Edward Crawford, Mother: Grace Taylor

Clair, Wm. Ellsworth — Male, September 11, 1906, Buxton, Iowa, Father: Chas. Elsworth Clair, Mother: Lizzie Jones

Carlson, Carl Wilford — Male, August 9, 1906, Buxton, Iowa, Father: Gust Carlson, Mother: Mary Larson

Curnikshank, Margaret Helen — Female, August 12, 1906, Buxton, Iowa, Father: Daniel Curnikshank, Mother: Annie Davis

Carlson, Henry Randolph — Male, March 16, 1907, Buxton, Iowa, Father: Carl Otto Carlson, Mother: Emma Louisa Carlson (No Maiden Name Given)

PAGE 77:
Cassells, George Sylvester — Male, July 28, 1907, Buxton, Iowa, Father: Mark Cassells, Mother: Luella Bennett

Cross, Emma — Female, May 31, 1907, Buxton, Iowa, Father: C.H. Cross, Mother: Hattie E. Lucas

Calvert, Clay Edward — Male, August 30, 1907, Buxton, Iowa, Father: Robert Calvert, Mother: Viola Alice Church

Calvert, Bessie — Female, July 26, 1907, Buxton, Iowa, Father: Robert Calvert, Mother: Della Bath

PAGE 78:
Clair, Edward John — Male, May 22, 1908, Buxton, Iowa, Father: Chas. Edward Clair, Mother: Elizabeth Jones

PAGE 79:
Carlson, Belinda Caroline — Female, February 14, 1906, Buxton, Iowa, Father: Carl A. Carlson, Mother: Olga Charlotta Anderson

Christensen, Kenneth — Male, April 19, 1906, Buxton, Iowa, Father: Alfred Christensen, Mother: Adell May Wortman

PAGE 103:
Downs, Mary Ellen — Female, February 26, 1902, Buxton, Iowa, Father: Edwin Ellsworth Downs, Mother: Martha Isabelle Carter

Douglass, Golda Essdoorse — Female, October 18, 1903, Buxton, Iowa, Father: Wm. Douglass, Mother: Hattie Gray

PAGE 104:

Downs, Edith Alice — Female, July 12, 1906, Buxton, Iowa, Father: Edwin Ellsworth Downs, Mother: Martha Isabel Carter

Davis, Wm. Cornelius — Male, December 14, 1906, Buxton, Iowa, Father: Chas. Edward Davis, Mother: Sarah Frances Downey

Davis, Wilma Cornelia — Female, December 14, 1906, Buxton, Iowa, Father: Chas. Edward Davis, Mother: Sarah Frances Downey

PAGE 105:

Dempsey, Elaine — Female, July 23, 1908, Buxton, Iowa, Father: Aidsell Dempsey, Mother: Julia A. Wheeler

Downs, Roderick — Male, September 4, 1908, Buxton, Iowa, Father: Chas. Edward Downs, Mother: Frances Downey (last name may be Davis)

Downs, Frederick — Male, September 4, 1908, Buxton, Iowa, Father: Chas. Edward Downs, Mother: Frances Downey (last name may be Davis)

PAGE 130:

Ennestrom, Anna — Female, April 28, 1907, Buxton, Iowa, Father: Gust Ennestrom, Mother: Lenna Larson

Elder, Verla Maxine — Female, November 20, 1908, Buxton, Iowa, Father: John Elder, Mother: Bertha Viola Mott

PAGE 148:

Finley, Arnetta — Female, July 20, 1906, Buxton, Iowa, Father: Joseph Finley, Mother: Mary Poindexter

PAGE 172:

Graves, Florence Perlie — Female, November 4, 1901, Buxton, Iowa, Father: Jorden Graves, Mother: Mary Lizzie Daile

PAGE 173:

Gustaveson, Harry R. — Male, July 13, 1902, Buxton, Iowa, Father: Victor Edward Gustaveson, Mother: Gusta Polly Carlson

PAGE 174:

Graves, Mellie — Female, September 24, 1906, Buxton, Iowa, Father: Jno. Henry Graves, Mother: Belle King

Grant, Estella — Female, August 28, 1906, Buxton, Iowa, Father: John A. Grant, Mother: Mary Stevenson

Gustaveson, Jennie Marie — Female, December 23, 1906, Buxton, Iowa, Father: Otto Livick Gustaveson, Mother: Anna Lettie Anderson

Griffin, William Walter — Male, November 2, 1906, Buxton, Iowa, Father: Walter Scott Griffin, Mother: Fanny Mae Claver

Gillman, Clarence James — Male, February 26, 1907, Buxton, Iowa, Father: August Gillman, Mother: Maggie O. Chambers

Gustafson, Frank Edward — Male, October 6, 1907, Buxton, Iowa, Father: Frank Gust Gustafson, Mother: Hannah Elison

PAGE 175:

Giefir, Mary — Female, August 10, 1908, Buxton, Iowa, Father: Andy Giefir, Mother: Annis Camolko

Graves, Unnamed — Male, August 10, 1908, Buxton, Iowa, Father: Lee Graves, Mother: Helen Coles

PAGE 201:

Hawkins, Lucile — Female, October 10, 1902, Buxton, Iowa, Father: Henry James Hawkins, Mother: Isabella Vincent

Herrington, Caroline Elizabeth — Female, February 6, 1902, Buxton, Iowa, Father: Matthew Patterson Herrington, Mother: Mary Elizabeth Myer

PAGE 203:

Hill, Vermont Lee — Male, July 31, 1906, Buxton, Iowa, Father: Charley Lee Hill, Mother: Laura Gaines

Hyatt, Edith Marie — Female, December 4, 1907, Buxton, Iowa, Father: Frank Willard Hyatt, Mother: Gertrude Hattie Sholly

Harris, Rosa Belle — Female, October 16, 1906, Buxton, Iowa, Father: John Wm. Harris, Mother: Gabrella Bryant

Harris, Floyd Mansier — Male, December 14, 1906, Buxton, Iowa, Father: Anderson Chas. Harris, Mother: Ada Long

Higgins, Lucile — Female, October 11, 1906, Buxton, Iowa, Father: Plumer Higgins, Mother: Mabel Claborn

PAGE 204:

Hawkins, Henry James — Male, December 7, 1907, Buxton, Iowa, Father: Hnery James Hawkins, Mother: Isabelle Vincent

PAGE 205:

Hart, Syble Maryline — Female, November 25, 1908, Buxton, Iowa, Father: Robert Hart, Mother: Ella Blackburn

Hurst, Nettie — Female, November 22, 1908, Buxton, Iowa, Father: A.C. Hurst, Mother: Lula Hammond

Holmes, John Valier — Male, August 22, 1908, Buxton, Iowa, Father: J.B. Holmes, Mother: Ethel B. Johnes

PAGE 206:

Hastings, George Henry Clay — Male, May 25, 1906, Buxton, Iowa, Father: James Henry Hastings, Mother: Anna Pearl Flanders

PAGE 249:

Isaacson, Carl Harry — Male, November 19, 1906, Buxton, Iowa, Father: Charley Augustiff Isaacson, Mother: Mary Ann Fisher

Ingnell, Alma Lennea — Female, October 22, 1907, Buxton, Iowa, Father: Carl John Emanuel Ingnell, Mother: Alma Olson

PAGE 260:

Jackson, Jenneta Isadora — Female, January 6, 1902, Buxton, Iowa, Father: Andre Richard Jackson, Mother: Mary Etta Collins

Jackson, Mary Frances — Female, March 3, 1902, Buxton, Iowa, Father: Jim Jackson, Mother: Sarah Bryan

Johnson, Ruth Marie — Female, April 9, 1902, Buxton, Iowa, Father: Charley J. Johnson, Mother: Tekla Josephine Flodman

PAGE 261:

Jones, Grace — Female, September 28, 1906, Buxton, Iowa, Father: Morris Wm. Jones, Mother: Meta Erickson

Janger, Christina — Female, October 7, 1906, Buxton, Iowa, Father: Michael Janger, Mother: Anna Hudak

Jones, Delissa Marie — Female, August 25, 1906, Buxton, Iowa, Father: John James Jones, Mother: Mamie Edgar

Jacob, James Arthur — Male, August 15, 1906, Buxton, Iowa, Father: James Jacob, Mother: Anna Gammary

Jones, Lorenzo Joseph — Male, October 18, 1906, Buxton, Iowa, Father: Henry Jones, Mother: Cleo Dorsey

Jones, Sarah — Female, June 29, 1907, Buxton, Iowa, Father: Floyd Jones, Mother: Eliza Hoggsette

Johnson, Marie Matilda — Female, December 15, 1907, Buxton, Iowa, Father: Carl Edward Johnson, Mother: Bertha Elfreda Larson

Jones, Susie Louise — Female, July 20, 1907, Buxton, Iowa, Father: Edward Franklin Jones, Mother: Daisy Ellen Wilson

PAGE 262:

Johnson, Gilbert Edwin — Male, May 29, 1908, Buxton, Iowa, Father: Carl Jno. Johnson, Mother: Anna Theresa Lundblad

Jones, Oscar Wm. Herbert — Male, July 30, 1908, Buxton, Iowa, Father: J.J. Jones, Mother: Maud Claburn

PAGE 276:

Kocur, Stephen — Male, July 3, 1906, Buxton, Iowa, Father: John Kocur, Mother: Anna Kris

Kovhn, Anna — Female, July 10, 1907, Buxton, Iowa, Father: Steve Kovhr, Mother: Agnes Benahn

King, Corina Matilda — Female, April 23, 1907, Buxton, Iowa, Father: Charles C. King, Mother: Arre Ann Josephine Carter

PAGE 277:

Koleson, Mary — Female, August 20, 1908, Buxton, Iowa, Father: George Koleson, Mother: Anna Gaclia

PAGE 297:

Long, Margaret Isabelle — Female, August 12, 1901, Buxton, Iowa, Father: Edward Thomas Long, Mother: Jennie Gordon

Lucas, Steve — Male, August 16, 1901, Buxton, Iowa, Father: Steve Lucas, Mother: Lizzie Sesock

PAGE 299:

Loury, Harry Ovilla — Male, December 6, 1902, Buxton, Iowa, Father: Lewis Loury, Mother: Mimarie Charlotte Coles

PAGE 300:

Larson, Levi — Male, August 3, 1906, Buxton, Iowa, Father: Lars John Larson, Mother: Augusta Olivia Hulteen

Larson, Arthur Edwin — Male, March 9, 1907, Buxton, Iowa, Father: Gust S. Larson, Mother: Ida Anderson

Larson, Einer Rutger — Male, September 23, 1907, Buxton, Iowa, Father: Axel Linus Larson, Mother: Clara Maria Blomgren

Leiby, J. Emery — Male, June 8, 1907, Buxton, Iowa, Father: Louis Sylvester Leiby, Mother: Maggie Latisha Reeser

PAGE 301:
Lewis, Mary Elizabeth — Female, January 22, 1908, Buxton, Iowa, Father: Wm. Preston Lewis, Mother: Mary Belle Carr

Lenger, Celina — Female, May 21, 1908, Buxton, Iowa, Father: Michael Lenger, Mother: Anna Haydeck

Lynch, Charles — Male, October 15, 1908, Buxton, Iowa, Father: Frank Lunch, Mother: Cora Garrison

Lucas, Joe — Male, September 29, 1906, Buxton, Iowa, Father: Joe Lucas, Mother: Lizzie Durbala

Larson, Harold Emanuel — Male, May 17, 1906, Buxton, Iowa, Father: John Fred Larson, Mother: Sophia Nelson

PAGE 327:
Mease, Laythan Elizabeth — Female, August 17, 1901, Buxton, Iowa, Father: Charles Henry Mease, Mother: Cornelia Francis Tate

PAGE 328:
Mathews, Charlie — Male, May 12, 1902, Buxton, Iowa, Father: Sam Mathews, Mother: Delia Irvins

PAGE 330:
Massey, Laisaint L. — Male, July 5, 1906, Buxton, Iowa, Father: Nicholas Reuben Massey, Mother: Zeffer Gertrude Jones

Miller, Inez Lenora — Female, July 5, 1906, Buxton, Iowa, Father: Lewis Miller, Mother: Florence Iren

Miller, George — Male, November 8, 1906, Buxton, Iowa, Father: George A. Miller, Mother: Pearl Ward

PAGE 332:

Morgan, Wm. Thaddeus B. — Male, August 20, 1908, Buxton, Iowa, Father: Wm. Morgan, Mother: Ella Pigg

Miller, Joseph Kenneth — Male, December 27, 1908, Buxton, Iowa, Father: Joseph Miller, Mother: Maud Covey

Morrell, Dorothy May — Female, March 25, 908, Buxton, Iowa, Father: John Morrell, Mother: Julia Taylor

Mease, Quentin — Male, October 25, 1908, Buxton, Iowa, Father: Chas. H. Mease, Mother: Cornelia F. Tate

PAGE 372:

McCully, Margaret Ann — Female, December 18, 1902, Buxton, Iowa, Father: Thomas McCulley, Mother: Phebe Jane Edwards

PAGE 373:

McKelvier, Mildred Xavier — Female, September 1, 1907, Buxton, Iowa, Father: Samuel McKelvier, Mother: Amelia Cavelier

PAGE 374:

McGaughy, Thomas — Male, April 17, 1908, Buxton, Iowa, Father: Wm. McGaughy, Mother: Carrie Williams

PAGE 383:

Nevins, Bertha Ecil — Female, July 6, 1902, Buxton, Iowa, Father: John Emery Nevins, Mother: Thena Mabel Wigginton

PAGE 400:

Odem, Florence May — Female, September 16, 1906, Buxton, Iowa, Father: Edward B. Odem, Mother: Marion May Bowman

Olson, Edna Victoria — Female, April 2, 1907, Buxton, Iowa, Father: Richard Olson, Mother: Tekla Josephine Nylander

PAGE 417:

Page, Orvil Lee — Male, February 26, 1902, Buxton, Iowa, Father: George Samuel Page, Mother: Mary Frances Powell

Phillips, Henry Wells — Male, April 24, 1902, Buxton, Iowa, Father: David Phillips, Mother: Mary Virginia Whitlock

PAGE 418:

Patterson, Ralph Ulysses — Male, December 3, 1906, Buxton, Iowa, Father: Wm. Michael Patterson, Mother: Fannie Fridlington

Peterson, Ida Caroline — Female, November 11, 1907, Buxton, Iowa, Father: Bent Carl Peterson, Mother: Anna Louisa Johnson

PAGE 419:

Pierce, Marcy — Female, April 14, 1908, Buxton, Iowa, Father: Wm. Richard Pierce, Mother: Ida E. King

Price, Unnamed — Male, July 12, 1908, Buxton, Iowa, Father: Frank Price, Mother: Monia Clark

PAGE 441:

Reeves, Okley May — Female, March 6, 1901, Buxton, Iowa, Father: Elicader Reeves, Mother: Fannie Brown

Rhodes, Albert Walter Rhodes — Male, August 29, 1902, Buxton, Iowa, Father: John Porter Rhodes, Mother: Rose Anna Daugherty

Rustan, Hilda — Female, December 9, 1902, Buxton, Iowa, Father: David Alian Rustan, Mother: Anna Anderson

Reisby, Louis — Male, December 9, 1902, Buxton, Iowa, Father: Louis Reisby Jr., Mother: Lucy Elizabeth Rogers

PAGE 443:

Rhoades, William Ardell — Male, November 23, 1906, Buxton, Iowa, Father: James Rhoades, Mother: Aldora Taylor

Robinson, George Calvin — Male, December 26, 1906, Buxton, Iowa, Father: Calvin Marshall Robinson, Mother: Lula Walters

Robinson, Alice — Female, October 15, 1906, Buxton, Iowa, Father: Lloyd Robinson, Mother: Miner Brown

Rhodes, Edward — Male, June 5, 1906, Buxton, Iowa, Father: William Brown Rhodes, Mother: Mary Ellen Ragsdale

Romster, Roy Earl — Male, July 20, 1907, Buxton, Iowa, Father: James Edward Romster, Mother: Rosa Ellen Goodwin

Reiplinger, Kathleen Elizabeth — Female, July 2, 1907, Buxton, Iowa, Father: Frank Henry Reiplinger, Mother: Violet May Bradley

Reisby, Leonard Swan — Male, May 16, 1908, Buxton, Iowa, Father: Jesse Herndon Reisby, Mother: Massie Curry

Reasby, Harold Velton — Male, March 10, 1908, Buxton, Iowa, Father: Lewis Reasby, Mother: Lucy Elizabeth Boyers

PAGE 477:
Serock, Margrette — Female, June 9, 1902, Buxton, Iowa, Father: Carl Serock, Mother: Mary Damack

Sears, Robert Miller — Male, January 6, 1902, Buxton, Iowa, Father: Jesse Miller Sears, Mother: Eliza Jane Cousin

Smith, Lillian May — Female, October 18, 1902, Buxton, Iowa, Father: Ferdenand A. Smith, Mother: Lovie Waddel Bumgarden

PAGE 480:
Swanson, Carl — Male, December 23, 1906, Buxton, Iowa, Father: Edward Swanson, Mother: Hannah Louisa Anderson

PAGE 481:
Smith, Georgia May — Female, November 11, 1907, Buxton, Iowa, Father: William Barney Smith, Mother: Anna Griffin

Sharp, Clifton B. — Male, October 5, 1907, Buxton, Iowa, Father: William Sharp, Mother: Lucy Black

Sivak, Lena — Female, August 6, 1907, Buxton, Iowa, Father: Steve Sivak, Mother: Lena Koohn

Sivak, Maria — Female, August 6, 1907, Buxton, Iowa, Father: Steve Sivak, Mother: Lena Koohn

Sears, Viola Dorothy — Female, September 25, 1907, Buxton, Iowa, Father: Jesse Miller Sears, Mother: Eliza Jane Cozzins

Shelton, Lilian Catherine — Female, September 14, 1907, Buxton, Iowa, Father: Charles Clinton Shelton, Mother: Mary Alice Berries

Smith, Leslie — Male, April 20, 1907, Buxton, Iowa, Father: Daniel M. Smith, Mother: Anna Martin

Stewart, Nalva — Female, May 30, 1907, Buxton, Iowa, Father: George Stewart, Mother: Betty Larkin

PAGE 482:

Server, Archie Edward — Male, June 16, 1908, Buxton, Iowa, Father: Edward Server, Mother: Ada Server (No Maiden Name Given)

Smith, Ernest Luther — Male, January 24, 1908, Buxton, Iowa, Father: Ferdinand Smith, Mother: Lovie Wadell Bumgarden

Sampson, Lillian Margaret — Female, May 30, 1908, Buxton, Iowa, Father: Chas. Jno. Sampson, Mother: Alta May Bringman

Smith, Oliver Edward — Male, November 6, 1908, Buxton, Iowa, Father: James Murray Smith, Mother: Isabella Robinson

Shepherd, Alfred Franklin — Male, August 24, 1908, Buxton, Iowa, Father: Joseph William Shepherd, Mother: Mary Lou Martin

PAGE 483:

Southard, Thos. Richard — Male, March 13, 1908, Buxton, Iowa, Father: Robert Southard, Mother: Anna Winsey

Summers, Alma Gertrude — Female, May 20, 1908, Buxton, Iowa, Father: Elijah Smith Summers, Mother: Elizabeth Ann Pierce

PAGE 533:

Turner, Hester Roxine — Female, December 16, 1906, Buxton, Iowa, Father: Wm. Edward Turner, Mother: Eunice Kenedy

Tate, Irma Electra — Female, October 1, 1906, Buxton, Iowa, Father: Benjamin Franklin Tate, Mother: Edna Virginia Ampy

Thomas, Claude Delmas — Male, March 15, 1907, Buxton, Iowa, Father: Harvey William Thomas, Mother: Bessie Edith Humphrey

PAGE 534:

Tate, Helena — Female, March 19, 1908, Buxton, Iowa, Father: Joseph Tate, Mother: Lydia Gibson

Tate, Junis Austin — Male, August 10, 1908, Buxton, Iowa, Father: Wm. Alex Tate, Mother: Emma Francis

Turner, Eunice C. — Female, December 5, 1908, Buxton, Iowa, Father: Wm. Turner, Mother: Eunice Kenedy

Taylor, Marvin — Male, September 6, 1908, Buxton, Iowa, Father: Louis Taylor, Mother: Frances Harvey

Turner, Zelma — Female, April 10, 1908, Buxton, Iowa, Father: James Turner, Mother: Lucy Bennett

PAGE 567:

Vance, William Webster — Male, February 20, 1902, Buxton, Iowa, Father: William Vincent Vance, Mother: Augusta Johnson

PAGE 568:

Van Arsdale, Laura Belle — Female, May 27, 1908, Buxton, Iowa, Father: G.W. Van Arsdale, Mother: Leder Branan

PAGE 575:

Wilcox, James Robert — Male, September 17, 1900, Buxton, Iowa, Father: Samuel Wilcox, Mother: Mary Albertine Williams

Walker, Rosie Beatrice — Female, June 24, 1901, Buxton, Iowa, Father: Robert Lee Walker, Mother: Mary Rhodes

Wesley, Lionel Milton — Male, April 7, 1901, Buxton, Iowa, Father: James W. Wesley, Mother: Sarah Kenney

Washington, Bernice Margaret — Female, November 24, 1901, Buxton, Iowa, Father: James Thomas Washington, Mother: Blanch V. White

Wilson, James Arthur Franklin — Male, February 23, 1901, Buxton, Iowa, Father: James Arthur Houston Garfield Wilson, Mother: Emma May Celia Ann Douglas

PAGE 578:

Wilson, Burrel Leonidas — Male, December 26, 1906, Buxton, Iowa, Father: Adolph Walter Wilson, Mother: Effie Pugh

Washington, Ester — Female, September 18, 1906, Buxton, Iowa, Father: James Washington, Mother: Isabella Branson

Woods, Mary Franklin — Female, December 8, 1906, Buxton, Iowa, Father: Frank Woods, Mother: Dollie Shepherd

Wilson, Lillian Augusta — Female, December 24, 1906, Buxton, Iowa, Father: Ernest Earl Wilson, Mother: Nellie Viola James

Wheels, Delbert Edgar — Male, December 7, 1906, Buxton, Iowa, Father: James Wheels, Mother: Katy Shade

Williams, Delma Vergil — Female, December 19, 1906, Buxton, Iowa, Father: Amos Williams, Mother: Myrtle Mary White

Webb, Andrew Vernon — Male, April 18, 1906, Buxton, Iowa, Father: Andrew Webb, Mother: Laura J. Campbell

Walker, Cornelius — Male, April 13, 1906, Buxton, Iowa, Father: Nelson W. Walker, Mother: Susie Victoria Arnold

Watkins, Unnamed — Female, January 29, 1907, Buxton, Iowa, Father: Samuel Watkins, Mother: Kansas Austin

Webb, Willard Ashby — Male, June 14, 1907, Buxton, Iowa, Father: Charles Washington Webb, Mother: Clara Dauson

Walden, Harry Spencer — Male, July 20, 1907, Buxton, Iowa, Father: Harry Walker Walden, Mother: Australia Carey

Washington, Harry Godfrey — Male, March 4, 1907, Buxton, Iowa, Father: William Washington, Mother: Mary Frances Stribling

Wells, Marvin Coffman — Male, November 28, 1907, Buxton, Iowa, Father: W. P. Wells, Mother: Kate Coffman

PAGE 579:

Washington, Unnamed — Male, July 17, 1908, Buxton, Iowa, Father: Jas. Henry Washington, Mother: Isabelle Branson

Walker, Naomi — Female, December 11, 1908, Buxton, Iowa, Father: Nelson Walker, Mother: Susie Arnold

Winkler, Teressa — Female, January 26, 1908, Buxton, Iowa, Father: Lucas Winkler, Mother: Teressa Fisty

Odessa Booker is shown with her scrapbook of articles, photos, and memories of her girlhood in Buxton. At right is an article about her experiences there.

Life in the 'black town' of Buxton

One phenomenon of black history in Iowa was the so-called black town — where, unlike today, blacks outnumbered the whites who lived there.

The place that comes most quickly to mind in such cases is Buxton, a booming Monroe County coal-mining town in the early 1900s that was home to between 6,000 and 8,000 residents, as many as 80 percent of them blacks.

Most of the residents were black miners, but Buxton also boasted black doctors, black lawyers, black teachers, black school board members, a black postmaster and a black justice of the peace.

Odessa Booker, now 80, recalls that era.

Booker rode up from Arkansas in 1904 at the age of 3 in the caboose of a train.

In Buxton, she remembers the parades, watching the black baseball team, the Buxton Wonders, and dancing the Charleston at the Sharp Inn nightclub where she wore elbow-length gloves and a beaded dress that she still owns.

Her father was killed in a mine accident so she quit school and "had to be a second mom, being the oldest child," and helped raise her brothers and sisters. "I hardly got to play with the other kids," she recalled.

Booker recalls earning $1.50 a week in a job at Buxton. "That was a lot of money then," she said. She also recalls how her mother stretched a scarce money supply — 25 cents provided a meal that "fed us all," Booker said.

The best thing she remembers about Buxton was that "everyone was so friendly. Nobody knew color or showed any partiality."

The family came to Des Moines in 1918 because there was no junior high school in Buxton. There Booker encountered prejudice — a different kind of prejudice common to blacks at the time.

"I came up here [to Des Moines] and couldn't find a job. They said I was too short for this and too little for that." She was 4 feet, 8 inches tall and weighed 89 pounds.

After she was married, she did find a job as an elevator operator. "I struggled but I made it," she said.

Monroe County, Iowa Birth Book 3
1909 - 1915

Information recorded:
This county record book of births includes child's name, race, sex, birth date, father's name, race, age, birth place, occupation of father, mother's name, race, age, birth place, children born to mother and number of children still living. The page number of the record book where the birth is recorded has been included for the convenience of researchers.

PAGE 1:
Antolik, Mabel Helen: White, Female, Born: September 3, 1909
Father: Antolik, Steve — White, Age 31, Born: Austria, Coal Miner
Mother: Chinko, Elizabeth — White, Age: 29, Born: Austria, 5 children born and 5 living.

Anderson, Marie: White, Female, Born: December 19, 1910
Father: Anderson, Elmer — White, Age 19, Born: Iowa, Miner
Mother: Sherbine, Grace — White, Age 19, Born: Illinois, 2 children born and 1living

PAGE 2:
Antolik, Albert: White, Male, Born: August 21, 1911
Father: Antolik, Steve — White, Age 35, Born: Austria, Miner
Mother: Chunko, Lizzie — White, Age 31, Born: Austria, 6 children born and 6 living

Antol, Annie: White, Female, Born: February 27, 1911
Father: Antol, George — White, Age 39, Born: Austria, Miner
Mother: Kapko, Mary — White, Age 33, Born: Austria, 6 children born and 4 living

Anderson, Clyde Vernon: Black, Male, Born: August 23, 1911
Father: Anderson, Frank — Black, Age 49, Born: Illinois, Miner Mother: Chapman, Lulu — Black, Age 36, Born: Missouri, 7 children born and 6 children living
(This record was amended later in Pima, Arizona. Name was amended to Anderson, William Estell and birth date was amended to July 20, 1913)

Anderson, Raymond Harold: White, Male, Born: December 10, 1912
Father: Anderson, Raymond Harold — White, Age 29, Born: Sweden, Miner
Mother: Bloomgren, Mary — White, Age 21, Born: Iowa, 1 child born and 1 living

Armstrong, Homer Carroll: White, Male, Born: February 23, 1912
Father: Armstrong, Victor — White, Age 22, Born: Iowa, Butcher
Mother: Schwartz, Rosa — White, Age 20, Born: Austria, 1 child born and 1 living

PAGE 4:
Allen, Wayne Edward: White, Male, Born: September 19, 1914
Father: Allen, Miles — White, No Age Given, Born: Iowa, Coal Miner
Mother: Code, Effie Mae — White, Age 20, Born: Austria, 1 child born and 1 living

PAGE 5:
Burkett, Clifford: Black, Male, Born: November 18, 1909
Father: Burkett, Philip Henry — Black, Age 30, Born: Virginia, Coal Miner
Mother: Wheeler, Mary Elizabeth — Black, Age 27, Illinois, 6 children born and 5 living

Beno, George: White, Male, Born: November 29, 1909
Father: Beno, Andy — White, Age 27, Born: Austria, Coal Miner
Mother: Hudak, Anna — White, Age 26, Born: Austria, 4 children born and 3 living

Bryson, Stella: Black, Female, Born: February 7, 1909
Father: Bryson, Sherman Wm. — Black, Age 46, Born: North Carolina, Justice of Peace
Mother: White, Maggie — Black, Age 35, Born: Vermont, 12 children born and 11 living

Betson, Wanda Bernice: White, Female, Born: April 29, 1909
Father: Betson, Fred — White, Age 38, Born: Illinois, Coal Miner
Mother: Williams, Mary — White, Age 24, Born: Wales, 2 children born and 1 living

Babcock, Dolly: White, Female, Born: September 9, 1909
Father: Babcock, Roy Arthur — White, Age 28, Born: Minnesota, Master Mechanic
Mother: Casselman, Florence May — White, Age 24, Born: Wisconsin, 4 children born and 3 living

Brooks, Joseph: Black, Male, Born: November 23, 1909
Father: Brooks, William — Black, Age 34, Born: Virginia, Blacksmith
Mother: Harrell, Sally — Black, Age 28, Born: North Carolina, 7 children born and 6 living

PAGE 6:

Barker, John E.: Black, Male, Born: July 21, 1910
Father: Barker, John — Black, Age 25, Born: Virginia, Miner
Mother: Fields, Minnie — White, Age 36, Born: Missouri, 3 children born and 2 living

Brookin, Edna E.: Black, Female, Born: October 22, 1910
Father: Brookin, Andrew J. — Black, Age 27, Born: Missouri, Railroad
Mother: Walker, Emil — Black, Age 23, Born: Iowa, 1 child born and 1living

Brown, Charles: White, Male, Born: August 5, 1910
Father: Brown, Charles — White, Age 44, Born: Tennessee, Miner
Mother: Packard, Margaret — White, Age 40, Born: Tennessee, 8 children born and 8 living

Blackstone, Gayle: White, Female, Born: October 4, 1910
Father: Blackstone, Chas. L. — White, Age 34, Engineer
Mother: Ditch, Frances — White, Age 30, Born: Iowa, 3 children born and 3 living

PAGE 7:

Barnett, Violet: White, Female, Born: November 16, 1910
Father: Barnett, Orvil — White, Age 30, Born: (Not Given), Teamster
Mother: Ross, Mattie — White, Age 24, Born: Iowa, 2 children born and 2 living

Benge, Natalia: White, Female, Born: May 6, 1910
Father: Benge, P.R. — White, Age 34, Born: Iowa, Miner
Mother: Lane, M.E. — White, Age 29, Born: Iowa, 6 children born and 5 living

PAGE 8:

Baird, Charles: White, Male, Born: November 27, 1911
Father: Baird, Andrew — White, Age 30, Born: Austria, Miner
Mother: Kyduck, Annie — White, Age 28, Born: Austria, 5 children born and 4 living

Bregar, John: White, Male, Born: June 11, 1911
Father: Bregar, Frank — White, Age 34, Austria, Miner
Mother: Postotnik, Ivana — White, Age 34, Born: Austria, 3 children born and 3 living

Blakey, Hattie Mae: Black, Female, Born: February 5, 1911
Father: Blakey, Richard — Black, Age 35, Born: Virginia
Mother: Burkett, Mary — Black, Age 30, Born: Virginia, 11 children born and 4 living

Barnett, Kenneth: White, Male, Born: July 5, 1911
Father: Barnett, James — White, Age 28, Born: Iowa
Mother: Culberson, Eva — White, Age 20, Born: Missouri, 2 children born and 2 living

Baxter, James: White, Male, Born: July 27, 1911
Father: Baxter, Neal — White, Age 21, Born: Iowa, Clerk
Mother: Messinger, Lula — White, Age 21, Born: Colorado, 1 child born and 1 living

Bokros, Helen: White, Female, Born: June 10, 1911
Father: Bokros, John — White, Age 30, Born: Austria, Miner
Mother: Timko, Mary — White. Age 28, Born: Austria

PAGE 10:
Bjorklund, Anna Elizabeth: White, Female, Born: August 12, 1912
Father: Bjorklund, Emil — White, Age 35, Born: Sweden, Miner
Mother: Anderson, Amanda — White, Age 25, Born: Sweden, 4 children born and 4 living

Benge, Wilma: White, Female, Born: January 5, 1912
Father: Benge, Perry — White, Age 42, Born: Iowa, Miner
Mother: Lane, Magy — White, Age 37, Born: Iowa, 7 children and 6 living

Blakey, Robert: Black, Male, Born: December 8, 1912
Father: Blakey, Frank — Black, Age 31, Born: Iowa, Miner
Mother: Doyle, Letha — Black, Age 18, Born: Virginia, 1 child born and 1 living

Beaman, Mabel Odessa: Black, Female, Born: March 15, 1912
Father: Beaman, Archie — Black, Age 48, Born: Alabama, Miner
Mother: Boyd, Julia — Black, Age 32, Born: Missouri, 1 child born and 1 living

Boden, Worthey Carl: White, Male, Born: June 9, 1912
Father: Boden, George — White, Age 37, Born: Iowa, Clerk
Mother: Niel, Mary — White, Age 35, Born: Iowa, 3 children born and 3 living

Brewer, Alice Genevive: White, Female, Born: January 5, 1912
Father: Brewer, W.H. — White, Age 33, Born: Iowa, Clerk
Mother: Page, Pearl — White, Age 23, Born: Iowa, 1 child born and 1 living

Beno, Mike: White, Male, Born: October 11, 1912
Father: Beno, Mike — White, Age 58, Born: Austria, Clerk
Mother: Lucas, Annie — White, Age 33, Born: Austria, 3 children born and 3 living

Bonnetti, Pete: White, Male, Born: August 27, 1912
Father: Bonnetti, Fred — White, Age 27, Born: Italy, Miner
Mother: Gusina, Annie — White, Age 33, Born: Austria, 3 children born and 3 living

Bucket, Carl: Black, Male, Born: August 6, 1912
Father: Bucket, Robt. — Black, Age 20, Born: Iowa, Miner
Mother: Capuder, Susie — None, Age 17, Born: Virginia, 1 child born and 1 living

Buckle, Stanley: White, Male, Born: August 25, 1912
Father: Buckle, Ed — White, Age 30, Born: Illinois, Miner
Mother: Gibbons, Cora — White, Age 31, Born: Illinois, 4 children born and 4 living

Burkett, Mary: Black, Female, Born: December 8, 1912
Father: Burkett, Philip — Black, Age 33, Born: Virginia
Mother: Wheeler, Mary — Black, Age 30, Born: Illinois, 6 children born and 6 living

PAGE 12:
Burkett, Phil: Black, Male, Born: December 30, 1913
Father: Burkett, Philip — Black, Age 30, Born: Illinois, Miner
Mother: Wheeler, Mary — Black, Age 31, Born: Illinois

Brookins, Altha Naomie: Black, Female, Born: January 9, 1913
Father: Brookins, Andrew J. — Black, Age 27, Born: East St. Louis, Illinois, Miner
Mother: Walker, Eva — Black, Age 26, Born: Illinois, 2 children born and 2 living

Bowls, Mary Alice: Black, Female, Born: February 24, 1914
Father: Bowls, Robert — Black, Age 24, Born: Iowa, Miner
Mother: Lowery, Elsie — Black, Age 21, Born: Iowa, 1 child born and 1living

A view of Buxton's downtown stores, in the early 1900s. Unlike many company towns, Buxton allowed and encouraged other businesses which competed with the company store in supplying the residents' shopping needs.

PAGE 16:

Baxter, Wilbert: White, Male, Born: February 2, 1914
Father: Baxter, Corneluis Blackstone — White, Age: None, Born: Iowa, Clerk
Mother: Messenger, Lula May — White, Age 23, Born: Colorado, 2 children born and 2 living

Baker, Fred Maynard: White, Male, Born: January 20, 1914
Father: Baker, Fred Raymond — White, Age 21, Born: Iowa, Coal Miner
Mother: Bolton, Maggie May — White, Age 20, Born: Iowa, 1 child born and 1 living

Blakey, Petrol: Black, Female, Born: October 31, 1914
Father: Blakey, Frank — Black, Age 26, Born: Iowa, Coal Miner
Mother: Doyle, Letha — Black, Age 19, Born: Virginia, 2 children born and 2 living

Burkett, Unnamed: Black, Female, Born: August 27, 1914
Father: Burkett, Robert — Black, Age 20, Born: Iowa, Coal Miner
Mother: Carpenter, Susie — Black, Age 19, Born: Virginia, 2 children born and 2 living

Blakey, Charles Clinton: Black, Male, Born: April 26, 1914
Father: Blakey, John Amity — Black, Age 27, Born: Iowa, Coal Miner
Mother: Parkey, Lotty Osceola — Black, Age 21, Born: Kentucky, 1 child born and 1 living

Brewer, Helen Geraldine: White, Female, Born: December 10, 1914
Father: Brewer, Herbert Willard — White, Age 34, Born: Iowa, Clerk
Mother: Page, Pearl Leona — White, Age 25, Born: Iowa, 2 children born and 2 living

PAGE 17:
Clark, Iole: White, Female, Born: November 9, 1909
Father: Clark, Alex Calender — White, Age 28, Born: Iowa, Coal Miner
Mother: Chambers, Jessie — White, Age 23, Born: Iowa, 3 children born and 3 children living

Calloway, Alphonson: Black — Illegitimate, Male, March 28, 1909
Father: Jones, John Henry — Black, Age 58, Born: Virginia, Coal Miner
Mother: Calloway, Martha — Black, Age 25, Born: Missouri, 4 children born and 4 living

Creach, Evaline: Black, Female, Born: No Date 1909
Father: Creach, Bert — Black, Age 27, Born: Tennessee, Coal Miner
Mother: Hubbard, Bernetta — Black, Age 22, Born: Kentucky, 1 child born and 1 living

PAGE 19:
Crute, James D.: Black, Male, Born: February 2, 1910
Father: Crute, Richard — Black, Age 35, Born: Virginia, Miner
Mother: Parker, Zella — Black, Age 23, Born: Virginia, 1 child born and 1 living

Colhar, Mike: White, Male, Born: May 3, 1910
Father: Colhar, John — White, Age 37, Born: Austria, Miner
Mother: Kupnes, Mary — White, Age 29, Born: Austria, 5 children born and 5 living

PAGE 20:
Carter, Celesta: Black, Female, Born: February 26, 1910
Father: Carter, John — Black, Age 26, Born: Iowa, Miner
Mother: Beamer, Iva — Black, Age 23, Born: Alabama, 2 children born and 2 living

Clair, Robert G.: White, Male, Born: May 28, 1910
Father: Clair, Charles E. — White, Age 28, Born: Iowa, Miner
Mother: Jones, Lizzie — White, Age 21, Born: Wyoming, 3 children born and 3 living

Carlson, Ralph: White, Male, Born: August 31, 1911
Father: Carlson, Gus — White, Age 35, Born: Sweden, Miner
Mother: Larson, Mary — White, Age 30, Born: Iowa, 3 children born and 3 living

PAGE 21:
Cooper, Jennie: White, Female, Born: September 30, 1911
Father: Cooper, Ervine — White, Age 27, Born: Iowa, Carpenter
Mother: Smith, Lonnie — White, Age 20, Born: Iowa, 1 child born and 1 living

Clark, Ellsworth: White, Male, Born: November 9, 1911
Father: Clark, Alexander — White, Age 29, Born: Iowa, Miner
Mother: Chambers, Jessie — White, Age 26, Born: Iowa, 4 children born and 4 living

Carlson, Rudolph: White, Male, Born: March 27, 1911
Father: Carlson, John H. — White, Age 34, Born: Sweden, Miner
Mother: Carlson, Alma — White, Age 36, Born: Sweden, 5 children born and 5 living

Cole, Thomas R.: White, Male, Born: June 7, 1911
Father: Cole, T.R. — White, Age 32, Born: Iowa, Bank Cashier
Mother: Tucker, Alice — White, Age 30, Born: Iowa, 1 child born and 1 child living

PAGE 23:
Corum, Unnamed: White, Male, Born: August 23, 1912
Father: Corum, Wm. Edward — White, Age 26, Born: Iowa. Miner
Mother: Gordon, Bertha — White, Age 24, Born: Missouri, 2 children born and 2 children living

Compestine, Amedo: White, Male, Born: September 24, 1912
Father: Compestine, Amedo — White, Age 29, Born: Austria, Miner
Mother: Anesi, Calterina — White, Age 24, Born: Austria, 6 children born and 3 children living

Clair, Goldie Gertrude: White, Female, Born: June 23, 1912
Father: Clair, Leslie Thomas — White, Age 20, Born: Kansas, Miner
Mother: Cooper, Nettie — White, Age 25, Born: Iowa, 1 child born and 1 child living

Cooper, Alwilda Mae: White, Female, Born: December 25, 1912
Father: Cooper, James — White, Age 21, Born: Iowa, Miner
Mother: Gustin, Maude — White, Age 16, Born: Iowa, 1 child born and 1 living

Carr, Mayetta: Black, Female, Born: August 21, 1912
Father: Carr, Geo. — Black, Age 25, Born: Iowa, Miner
Mother: Robinson, Francis — Black, Age 21, Born: Iowa, 2 children born and 2 living

Carlson, Glen Gust: White, Male, Born: July 19, 1912
Father: Carlson, Gust — White, Age 38, Born: South Carolina, Miner
Mother: Larson, Mary — White, Age 32, Born: Iowa, 4 children born and 4 living

Colberg, Hilda Christina: White, Female, Born: June 8, 1912
Father: Colberg, Chas. — White, Age 30, Born: Sweden, Miner
Mother: Swanson, Mandy — White, Age 25, Born: Iowa, 1 child born and 1 living

Cappellin, Marry: White, Female, Born: May 24, 1912
Father: Cappellin, John — White, Age 25, Born: Italy, Miner
Mother: Delpiere, Charlotte — White, Age 17, Born: France, 1 child born and 1 living

PAGE 24:
Cross, August: Black, Male, Born: August 6, 1912
Father: Cross, C.H. — Black, Age 35, Born: Kentucky, Miner
Mother: Lucas, Lizzie — Black, Age 40, Born: Kentucky, 14 children born and 8 living

Catho, John: White, Male, Born: May 31, 1912
Father: Catho, Geo. — White, Age 29, Born: Austria, Miner
Mother: Berto, Emma — White, Age 20, Born: Iowa, 1 child born and 1 child living

PAGE 27:

Day, Bernice Edith: White, Female, Born: December 7, 1909
Father: Day, George H. — White, Age 33, Born: Iowa, Teamster
Mother: Robinson, Winnie F. — White, Age 28, Born: Iowa, 2 children born and 2 living

Davis, Olive May: White, Female, Born: December 5, 1909
Father: Davis, George — White, Age 35, Born: England, Miner
Mother: Moses, Elizabeth Lavinia — White, Age 30, Born: Wales

PAGE 28:

Dabney, Mildred: Black, Female, Born: May 21, 1910
Father: Dabney, Charles — Black, Age 29, Born: Virginia, Miner
Mother: Cobb, Hallie — Black, Age 20, Born: Virginia, 1 child born and 1 living

Davis, Gerald Raymond: Black, Male, Born: December 2, 1910
Father: Davis, Chas. E. — Black, Age 37, Born: Iowa, Miner
Mother: Downey, Francis — Black, Age 24, Born: Iowa, 7 children born and 6 living

PAGE 29:

Dobes, Mary: White, Female, Born: December 10, 1911
Father: Dobes, George — White, Age 29, Born: Austria, Miner
Mother: Cornick, Julia — White, Age 25, Born: Austria. 5 children born and 4 living

Dempsey, Edward W.: White, Male, Born: May 15, 1911
Father: Dempsey, A.S. — White, Age 31, Born: Ohio, Electrician
Mother: Wheeler, Julia — White, Age 26, Born: Kentucky, 2 children born and 2 living

PAGE 30:

Donavick, Vance: White, Male, Born: July 12, 1912
Father: Donavick, August — White, Age 29, Born: Italy, Miner
Mother: Cremk, Julius — White, Age 25, Born: Italy, 3 children born and 3 living

Deering, Howard William: Black, Male, Born: May 18, 1912
Father: Deering, Handy — Black, Age 26, Born: Virginia, Miner
Mother: Simmons, Mamie — Black, Age 17, Born: North Carolina, 2 children born and 1 living

The home of John Blomgren, Sr., located in East Swedetown (a section of Buxton, Iowa). The house was built in 1906. Left to right: Esther, Emanual, Anna, Art, Carl, Rose, Alf and father John Blomgren.

PAGE 36:

Engstrom, Naomi: White, Female, Born: March 11, 1909
Father: Engstrom, Gust — White, Age 31, Born: Sweden, Coal Miner
Mother: Larson, Rena — White, Age 34, Born: Sweden, 7 children born and 7 living

Estes, Traister: White, Male, Born: December 9, 1910
Father: Estes, James — White, Age 46, Born: Kentucky, Miner
Mother: Mc Coy, Lydia — White, Age 37, Born: Kansas, 3 children born and 3 living

Edwards, Olive: White, Female, Born: June 18, 1910
Father: Edwards, L.M. — White, Age 36, Born: Iowa, Miner
Mother: Bolden, Hazel — White, Age 23, Born: Kansas, 2 children born and 2 living

PAGE 37:
Elder, Ralph: White, Male, Born: August 10, 1912
Father: Elder, John — White, Age 32, Born: Iowa, Fireman
Mother: Mott, Bertha — White, Age 27, Born: Iowa

Estoka, John: White, Male, Born: Not Given
Father: Estoka, John — White, Age 24, Born: Not Given, Miner
Mother: Not Given, Lizzie — White, Age 30, 2 children born and 2 living

PAGE 40:
Fowler, Beatrice: White, Female, Born: November 9, 1909
Father: Fowler, John — White, Age 35, Born: England, Miner
Mother: Dunn, Anna — White, Age 35, Born: England, 7 children born and 7 living

PAGE 41:
Frith, Theodore: Black, Male, Born: June 4, 1911
Father: Frith, J.G. — Black, Age 30, Born: Virginia, Miner
Mother: Bolden, Mamie — Black, Age 35, Born: Washington, D.C., 6 children born and 5 living

PAGE 42:
Freeman, Lola Lucille: White, Female, Born: June 15, 1911
Father: Freeman, C.J. — White, Age 34, Born: Iowa, Farmer
Mother: Hilliand, Mina — White, Age 28, Born: Iowa, 3 children born and 3 living

Franklin, Roberta Allen: Black, Female, Born: August 11, 1912
Father: Franklin, Robert Wm. — Black, Age 48, Born: Missouri, Miner
Mother: Allen, Cora — Black, Age 41, Born: Iowa, 7 children born and 5 living

Fathergill, Clantha: White, Female, Born: September 9, 1912
Father: Fathergill, Joe — White, Age 38, Born: England, Miner
Mother: Donavan, Goldy — White, Age 29, Born: Missouri, 2 children born and 2 living

Fowler, Ralph: White, Male, Born: February 10, 1912
Father: Fowler, John — White, Age 38, Born: England, Miner
Mother: Dunn, Annie — White, Age 38, Born: England, 8 children born and 8 living

PAGE 43:

Frencak, Joe: White, Male, Born: August 18, 1912
Father: Frencak, John — White, Age 35, Born: Austria, Miner
Mother: Frencak, Rosie — White, Age 26, Born: Austria, 4 children born and 4 living

PAGE 44:

Freeman, Naomi Minnie: Black, Female, Illegitimate, Born: September 10, 1914
Father: William, Charles — Black, Age 28, Born: Virginia, Miner
Mother: Freeman, Cora — Black, Age 22, Born: Tennessee, 3 children born and 2 living

PAGE 48:

Griffin, Marvin Mearl: White, Male, Born: May 10, 1909
Father: Griffin, Walter Scott — White, Age 26, Born: Iowa, Laborer
Mother: Claver, Fannie Mae — White, Age 18, Born: Iowa, 3 children born and 3 living

Garnett, Frank Wesley: Black, Male, Born: July 17, 1909
Father: Garnett, Wesley -- Black, Age 35, Born: Virginia, Coal Miner
Mother: Johnson, Anna Lavinia — Black, Age 22, Born: Iowa, 2 children born and 2 living

Gasper, George Tuban: White, Male, April 15, 1909
Father: Gasper, John — White, Age 36, Born: Austria, Coal Miner
Mother: Chuck, Barbary — White, Age 29, Born: Austria, 5 children born and 4 living

Gogo, John: White, Male, Born: July 26, 1909
Father: Gogo, George — White, Age 35, Born: Austria, Coal Miner
Mother: Hornak, Anna — White, Age 28, Born: Austria, 3 children born and 3 living

Griffin, Albert A.: White, Male, Born: December 15, 1910
Father: Griffin, Walter S. — White, Age 28, Born: Iowa
Mother: Claver, Fannie — White, Age 22, Born: Iowa, 4 children born and 4 living

PAGE 49:

Gustine, Eugene: White, Male, Born: June 6, 1911
Father: Gustine, W.E. — White, Age 46, Born: Kansas, Miner
Mother: Gause, Selia — White, Age 40, Born: Iowa, 11 children born and 9 children living

Gibbons, Eva: Black, Female, Born: July 6, 1911
Father: Gibbons, Thomas J. — Black, Age 21, Born: Iowa, Miner
Mother: Lewis, Ella — Black, Age 20, Born: Indiana Territory

PAGE 50:

Gibbons, Harold: White, Male, Born: September 28, 1911
Father: Gibbons, Edward — White, Age 22, Born: Iowa, Miner
Mother: Roberts, Rose M. — White, Age 19, Born: Iowa, 1 child born and 1 living

Garanch, Daniel: White, Male, Born: December 14, 1912
Father: Garanch, Paul — White, Age, 22, Born: Austria, Miner
Mother: Radosvich, Antonia — White, Age 26, Born: Austria, 2 children born and 1 living

Glankovic, Mary: White, Female, Born: September 15, 1912
Father: Glankovic, Andrew — White, Age 30, Born: Austria, Miner
Mother: Carnego, Annie — White, Age 25, Born: Iowa, 4 children born and 4 living

Griffin, Earl Freemont: White, Male, Born: January 7, 1912
Father: Griffin, Walter S. — White, Age 29, Born: Iowa
Mother: Claver, Fannie — White, Age 24, 5 children born and 4 living

Gulla, Martin: White, Male, Born: June 14, 1912
Father: Gulla, John — White, Age 38, Born: Austria, Miner
Mother: Hinnerrick, Ella — White, Age 32, Born: Austria, 7 children born and 7 living

Green, Anna: White, Female, Born: January 28, 1912
Father: Green, John — White, Age 33, Born: Russia
Mother: Chasnowothe, Mancka — White, Age 29, Born: Russia, 6 children born and 6 living

Graves, Zelma: Black, Female, Born: November 7, 1912
Father: Graves, John — Black, Age 55, Born: Virginia, Miner
Mother: King, Bell — Black, Age 40, Born: North Carolina, 8 children born and 8 living

PAGE 55:

Hogsett, Virginia: Black, Female, Illegitimate, Born: February 5, 1909
Father: Brown, Thomas — Black, Age 25, Born: Virginia, Coal Miner
Mother: Hogsett, Virginia — Black, Age 18, Born: Missouri, 1 child born and 1 living

Hogsett, Earl: Black, Male, Born: October 18, 1909
Father: Hogsett, Sherman — Black, Age 20, Born: Iowa, Coal Miner
Mother: Green, Eva — Black, Age 17, Born: Maryland, 1 child born and 1 living

Horn, Coleman Lawson: Black, Male, Born: March 22, 1909
Father: Horn, Charles Lawson — Black, Age 28, Born: Virginia, Coal Miner
Mother: Greever, Amanda — Black, Age 29, Born: Virginia, 1 child born and 1 living

Hawkins, Thomas: Black, Male, Born: December 7, 1909
Father: Hawkins, Henry — Black, Age 39, Born: Virginia, Coal Miner
Mother: Vircon, Isabella — Black, Age 30, Born: Iowa, 5 children born and 5 living

Holland, Andrew Robert: Black, Male, Born: May 31, 1909
Father: Holland, John — Black, Age 33, Born: Virginia, Coal Miner
Mother: Tansel, Sarah — Black, Age 37, Born: Alabama, 7 children born and 7 living

Hecker, Edward: White, Male, Born: October 2, 1909
Father: Hecker, Vincennes — White, Age 39, Born: Germany, Coal Miner
Mother: Essenger, Mary — White, Age 29, Born: Germany, 1 child born and 1 living

Houston, Letha: White, Female, Born: May 29, 1909
Father: Houston, Earl — White, Age 25, Born: Iowa, Coal Miner
Mother: Michel, Myrtle — White, Age 19, Born: Iowa, 1 child born and 1 living

Howard, Hubert: Black, Male, Born: July 19, 1909
Father: Howard, Andrew — Black, Age 28, Born: Ohio, Coal Miner
Mother: Harvey, Amanda — Black, Age 24, Born: Iowa

Hassko, Andrew: White, Male, Born: November 30, 1909
Father: Hassko, Joseph — White, Age 28, Born: Austria, Coal Miner
Mother: Gasper, Mary — White, Age 22, Born: Austria, 2 children born and 2 living

PAGE 56:

Hawkins, Ruth O.: White, Female, Born: April 10, 1910
Father: Hawkins, George — White, Age 28, Born: Missouri, Teamster
Mother: Jackson, ,Minnie — White, Age 21, Born: Iowa, 4 children born and 4 living

Hyatt, Roger W.: White, Male, Born: July 13, 1910
Father: Hyatt, Frank — White, Age 28, Born: Ohio, Clerk
Mother: Sholly, Gertie — White, Age 30, Born: Iowa, 3 children born and 3 living

PAGE 58:

Hockins, Mildred L.: White, Female, Born: August 11, 1911
Father: Hockins, Walter — White, Age 27, Born: Wales, Miner
Mother: Parkins, Lisebeth — White, Age 25, Born: England, 3 children born and 3 living

Harland, Edith N.: Black, Female, Born: January 9, 1911
Father: Harland, John — Black, Age 36, Born: Virginia, Miner
Mother: Tansel, Sarah — Black, Age 46, Born: Alabama, 8 children born and 8 living

Henley, Mae Lizzie: Black, Female, Born: September 19, 1911
Father: Henley, Joe — Black, Age 45, Born: North Carolina, Miner
Mother: Penelton, Rachel — Black, Age 35, Born: Virginia, 8 children born and 4 living

Hunter, Robert S.: Black, Male, Born: September 2, 1911
Father: Hunter, Lawrence — Black, Age 25, Born: Missouri, Miner
Mother: Cary, Mary — Black, Age 20, Born: Virginia, 2 children born and 2 living

PAGE 59:

Hubanks, Bertha: White, Female, Born: August 8, 1912
Father: Hubanks, Wm. — White, Age 41, Born: Iowa, Teamster
Mother: Isaacson, Hattie — White, Age Not Given, Born: Iowa, 3 children born and 2 living

Harris, Sarah Frances: White, Female, Born: June 19, 1912
Father: Harris, Herbert — White, Age 21, Born: Wales
Mother: Cooper, Bessie — White, Age 19, Born: Iowa, 1 child born and 1 living

Harper, Hattie: White, Female, January 6, 1912
Father: Harper, John — White, Age 52, Born: Iowa
Mother: Coffer, Clara -- White, Age 34, Born: Kentucky, 1 child born and 1 living

Hyatt, Frank W.: White, Male, Born: July 29, 1912
Father: Hyatt, Frank Willard — White, Age 30, Born: Ohio
Mother: Sholly, Gertrude Hattie — White, Age 31, Born: Illinois, 4 children born and 4 living

Holland, John H.: Black, Male, Born: December 18, 1912
Father: Holland, John Henry — Black, Age 36, Born: Virginia, Miner
Mother: Townsend, Sarah — Black, Age 40, Born: Alabama, 4 children born and 4 living

Harding, Fannie: White, Female, Born: September 9, 1912
Father: Harding, Henry — White, Age 30, Born: Iowa, Miner
Mother: Spangler, Ollie — White, Age 22, Born: Iowa, 1 child born and 1 living

Hesler, Rhody: White, Male, Born: September 10, 1912
Father: Hesler, Vinnecent — White, Age 42, Born: Austria
Mother: Essenger, Mary — White, Age 33, Born: Austria, 3 children born and 2 living

Hritz, Verna: White, Female, Born: December 20, 1912
Father: Hritz, John — White, Age 48, Born: Austria, Miner
Mother: Massage, Annie — White, Age 36, Born: Austria, 7 children born and 6 living

Hresko, Mary: White, Female, Born: January 16, 1912
Father: Hresko, Joe — White, Age 29, Born: Austria
Mother: Gasper, Mary — White, Age 25, Born: Austria, 3 children born and 3 living

PAGE 60:
Hunter, Lawrence: Black, Male, Born: February 17, 1913
Father: Hunter, Lawrence — Black, Age 28, Born: Virginia, Miner
Mother: Cary, Mary — Black, Age 22, Born: Virginia, 3 children born and 3 living

Hunt, J.C.: White, No gender given, Born: September 20, 1913
Father: Hunt, Geo. D. — White, Age 22, Born: Nebraska, Miner
Mother: Clair, Grace — White, Age 18, Born: Iowa, 1 child born and 1 living

The Monroe Mercantile Company (the company store operated by Consolidated Coal) burned to the ground in 1910. This photo shows the aftermath of the devastating fire. The original building was three full stories. It was rebuilt on a slightly-smaller scale and continued to provide everything from caskets to safety pins for Buxton's residents. The house on the horizon at upper right is the mine superintendent's home.

Hicks, Leona: White, Female, Born: No date given
Father: Hicks, Jeffrey — White, Age 31, Born: Illinois, Miner
Mother: Gustine, Gale — White, Age 23, Born: Knoxville, Iowa, 2 children born and 2 living

PAGE 61:
Hogshead, Mable: Black, Female, Born: January 26, 1913
Father: Hogshead, Sherman — Black, Age 30, Born: Not given
Mother: Roach, Mable — No race given, Age 24, Born: Buxton, Iowa

Hurst, Alvin: No race given, Male, Illegitimate, Born: March 19, 1914
Father: None given
Mother: Hurst, Lottie — No race given, No age given, No birthplace given

PAGE 63:
Hagglund, Anna Viola: White, Female, Born: October 4, 1914
Father: Hagglund, Albert — White, Age 26, Born: Iowa, Merchant
Mother: Blomgren, Betty — White, Age 21, Iowa, 2 children born and 2 living

Hawkins, Alace: Black, Female, Born: June 8, 1914
Father: Hawkins, Henry Clay — Black, Age 38, Born: Virginia, Coal Miner
Mother: Vianson, Isabelle — Black, Age 35, Born: Iowa, 7 children born and 5 living

Hudak, John: No information given
Father: Hudok, Steve — White, Age 25, Born: Austria, Coal Miner
Mother: Chonko, Tracy — White, Age 22, Born: Austria, 1 child born and 1 living

PAGE 65:
Ceglar, Steven: White, Male, Born: December 15, 1914
Father: Ceglar, Ignatz — White, Age 40, Born: Austria, Coal Miner
Mother: Turtnik, Frances — White, Age 35, Born: Austria, 9 children born and 4 living

PAGE 66:
Craft, Everet Duane: White, Male, Born: September 8, 1914
Father: Craft, Benjamin Harrison — White, Age 26, Born: South Dakota, Teamster
Mother: Pierce, Mary Etta — White, Age 22, Born: Iowa, 3 children born and 3 children living

Connor, David Oliver: White, Male, Born: November 14, 1914
Father: Connor, Asa B. — White, Age 36, Born: Illinois, Mechanic
Mother: Connor, Sibyl Nelson — White, Age 36, Born: Illinois, 2 children born and 2 living

Carter, Edward Albert: Black, Male, Born: September 23, 1914
Father: Carter, Edward Albert — Black, Age 33, Born: Virginia, Doctor
Mother: Warren, Rose Etta — Black, Age 28, Born: Ohio, 2 children born and 2 living

Church, Doris Irene: White, Female, Born: April 17, 1914
Father: Church, Edward Lawrence — White, Age 22, Born: Iowa, Coal Miner
Mother: Smith, Myrtle — White, Age 19, Born: Iowa, 1 child born and 1 living

Clark, Mary Maxine: White, Female, Born: July 24, 1914
Father: Clark, Alexander Cullinder — White, Age 23, Born: Iowa, Coal Miner
Mother: Chambers, Jessie — White, Age 28, Born: Iowa, 5 children born and 5 living

Carr, Odessa: Black, Female, Born: April 6, 1914
Father: Carr, George — Black, Age 28, Born: Iowa, Coal Miner
Mother: Robinson, Mary Francis — Black, Age 23, Born: Iowa, 3 children born and 2 living

Cooper, James Alfred: White, Male, Born: January 12, 1914
Father: Cooper, James Roy — White, Age 22, Born: Iowa, Teamster
Mother: Gustin, Maud — White, Age 19, Born: Iowa, 2 children born and 2 living

Chaney, Edward Theodore: No race given, Male, Born: July 28, 1913
Father: Chaney, Robert — No race or age given, Born: West Virginia
Mother: Harris, Maud — No race or age given, Born: New York

Calvert, Donald Eugene: No race given, Male, Born: July 28, 1913
Father: Calvert, Edward — No race or age given, Born: Illinois
Mother: Church, Viola Alice — No race or age given, Born: Iowa

Page 67:
Isaacson, Evelyn D.: White, Female, Born: September 16, 1910
Father: Isaacson, Charles — White, Age 49, Born: Sweden, Miner
Mother: Fisher, Mary — White, Age not given, Born: Illinois, 8 children born and 8 living

Page 70:
James, Elsie May: White, Female, Born: October 21, 1909
Father: James, Edwin — White, Age 27, Born: Ohio, Coal Miner
Mother: Curry, Nattie Elizabeth — White, Age 24, Born: Iowa, 2 children born and 2 living

Johnson, Everett A.: Black, Male, Born: September 2, 1909
Father: Johnson, William — Black, Age 29, Born: Ohio, Coal Miner
Mother: Gaines, Anna — Black, Age 25, Born: Iowa

PAGE 71:

Jones, Joseph Edward: White, Male, Born: October 4, 1910
Father: Jones, Eli B. — White, Age 24, Born: Illinois, Coal Miner
Mother: Plaet, Mary Etta — White, Age 28, Born: Ohio, 2 children born and 2 living

Jones, Alberta Birdie: Black, Female, Born: April 4, 1910
Father: Jones, Benjamin Sr. — Black, Age 28, Born: Virginia
Mother: Pollard, Lily — Black, Age 27, Born: Virginia, 12 children born and 7 living

Johnson, Rubey: White, Female, Born: October 19, 1910
Father: Johnson, Carl — White, Age 37, Born: Sweden, Miner
Mother: Lundbel, Annie — White, Age 31, Born: Sweden, 2 children born and 2 living

Jones, Martha L.: Black, Female, Born: September 24, 1910
Father: Jones, B.A. — Black, Age 23, Born: West Virginia, Miner
Mother: Willis, Evelyn — Black, Age 19, Born: Virginia, 1 child born and 1 living

Johnson, Christina: Black, Female, Born: April 4, 1911
Father: Johnson, R.J. — Black, Age 47, Born: Virginia, Miner
Mother: Wallace, Ella — Black, Age 23, Born: Iowa, 2 children born and 2 living

PAGE 72:

James, Ernest E.: White, Male, Born: February 15, 1912
Father: James, Ernest E. — White, Age 31, Born: Wales, Fireman
Mother: Jones, Mary Ann — White, Age 29, Born: Wales, 4 children born and 2 living

Jones, Mary Madline: Black, Female, Born: February 16, 1912
Father: Jones, Charles P. — Black, Age 31, Born: Iowa, Miner
Mother: Ellis, Lulu — Black, Age 27, Born: Iowa, 1 child born and 1 living

Jackson, Isadora Joseph: Black, Male, Born: April 16, 1912
Father: Jackson, John — Black, Age 57, Born: Virginia, Miner
Mother: Calaway, Martha — Black, Age 28, Born: Missouri, 4 children born and 4 living

Jennesson, Calvin: White, Male, Born: March 5, 1912
Father: Jennesson, Wm. S. — White, Age 57, Born: None given, Miner
Mother: Blackstone, Lizzie — White, Age 31, Norn: Iowa, 7 children born and 4 living

Johnson, Carl: Black, Male, Born: December 20, 1912
Father: Johnson, Ralph J. — Black, Age 46, Born: Virginia, Miner
Mother: Wallard, Ella — Black, Age 25, Born: Iowa, 3 children born and 3 living

Jacobson, Andrew: White, Male, Born: October 20, 1912
Father: Jacobson, Andrew — White, Age 29, Born: Austria, Miner
Mother: Vulgar, Barbara — White, Age 25, Born: Austria, 3 children born and 3 living

Jones, Adolph: Black, Male, Born: April 9, 1912
Father: Jones, Adolph — Black, Age 19, Born: Iowa, Miner
Mother: Brown, Alice — Black, Age 17, Born: Iowa, 4 children born and 4 living

James, Rosa Evelyn: Black, Female, Born: January 29, 1912
Father: James, B. — Black, Age 25, Born: West Virginia, Miner
Mother: Willis, Evelyn — Black, Age 21, Born: Virginia, 2 children born and 1 living

Jones, Leona M.: White, Female, Born: September 30, 1913
Father: Jones, Wm. --White, Age 43, Born: Wales, Foreman
Mother: Parry, Mattie — White, Age 32, Born: Iowa, 3 children born and 3 living

Jones, Florence Annie: White, Female, Born: October 2, 1913
Jones, Jas. R. — White, Age 31, Born: Not given, Coal Mining
Mother: Willey, Christina -- Race not given, Age 25, Born: Not given

Page 73:
Jones, Artholia: Black, Female, Born: November 25, 1913
Father: Jones, Henry — Black, Age 47, Born: Virginia, Miner
Mother: Stypes, Clio — Black, Age 33, Born: Illinois, 9 children born and 7 children living

Jones, Sylvia L. Ellis: Black, Female, Born: February 3, 1913
Father: Jones, R.T. — Black, Age not given, Born: Not given, Miner
Mother: Ellis, Mary — No information given

Jones, Charles R.: Black, Male, Born: July 1, 1913
Father: Jones, Chas. — Black, Age not given, Born: Not given, Coal Miner
Mother: Ellis, Tulla — Black, Age 28, Born: Iowa

Unidentified group of Buxton residents, undated.

PAGE 74:

Jones, Sarah Irene: White, Female, Born: December 13, 1914
Father: Jones, John C. — White, Age 50, Born: England, Coal Miner
Mother: Spangle, Lucinda — White, Age 36, Born: Iowa, 11 children born and 9 living

Koslior/ Koselar, Unnamed: White, Male, Born: October 12, 1909
Father: Koslior/ Koselar, George — White, Age 26, Born: Austria, Coal Miner
Mother: Koleo, Anna — White, Age 21, Born: Austria, 2 children born and 2 living

PAGE 75:

Kochevar, William: White, Male, Born: October 5, 1911
Father: Kochevar, Fred — White, Age 37, Born: Austria, Miner
Mother: Bartoll, Mary — White, Age 27, Born: Austria, 2 children born and 2 living

Kubashek, Frank Matthew: White, Male, Born: September 21, 1911
Father: Kubashek, Steve — White, Age 23, Born: Austria, Miner
Mother: Durbala, Annie — White, Age 18, Born: Iowa

Kocur, John: White, Male, Born: July 5, 1912
Father: Kocur, John — White, Age 39, Born: Austria, Miner
Mother: Kriss, Annie — White, Age 29, Born: Austria, 4 children born and 3 living

Koller, Unnamed: White, No gender given, Born: July 15, 1912
Father: Koller, George — White, Age 31, Born: Austria, Miner
Mother: Hreha, Mary — White, Age 21, Born: Iowa, 1 child born and 1 living

PAGE 76:

Kristof, Aabriela: White, Female, Born: March 4, 1912
Father: Kristof, Frank — White, Age 35, Born: Austria, Miner
Mother: Bajec, Helen — White, Age 25, Born: Austria, 3 children born and 3 living

Kry, Joe: White, Male, Born: November 12, 1912
Father: Kry, Joe — White, Age 22, Born: Italy, Miner
Mother: Kifer, Annie — White, Age 19, Born: Italy, 1 child born and 1 living

Kocur, George Daniel: White, Male, Born: January 27, 1912
Father: Kocur, George — White, Age 34, Born: Austria, Miner
Mother: Botson, Annie — White, Age 31, Born: Pennsylvania, 5 children born and 5 living

Kotush, Annie: White, Female, Born: March 4, 1912
Father: Kotush, Mike — White, Age 37, Born: Austria
Mother: Raspani, Susie — White, Age 30, Born: Austria, 4 children born and 4 living

PAGE 78:

Kristof, Mary Francis: White, Female, Born: January 29, 1914
Father: Kristof, Frank — White, Age 37, Born: Austria, Coal Miner
Mother: Bajec, Helen — White, Age 27, Born: Austria, 5 children born and 4 living

Kollar, Alvira Anne: White, Female, Born: February 19, 1914
Father: Kollar, George — White, Age 32, Born: Austria, Coal Miner
Mother: Hreka, Mary Lucy — White, Age 23, Born: Iowa, 2 children born and 1 living

Kubasek, Christina Agnes: White, Female, Born: August 2, 1914
Father: Kubasek, Steve — White, Age 27, Born: Austria
Mother: Durbala, Anna May — White, Age 21, Born: Iowa, 2 children born and 1 living

PAGE 79:

Linger/ Lenger, Charles: White, Male, Born: September 19, 1909
Father: Linger/ Lenger, Joseph — White, Age 26, Born: Hungary, Coal Miner
Mother: Mitrisin, Elizabeth — White, Age not given, Born: Pennsylvania, 1 child born and 1 living

Lewis, Helen Lenette: Black, Female, Born: August 11, 1909
Father: Lewis, William P. — Black, Age 32, Born: Virginia, Clerk
Mother: Carr, Mary Bell — Black, Age 34, Born: Virginia, 7 children born and 6 living

Leneze, Lois V.: White, Male, Born: February 14, 1910
Father: Leneze, Charles — White, Age 26, Born: Iowa, Coal Miner
Mother: Henry Lizzie — White, Age 20, Born: Iowa, 2 children born and 2 living

PAGE 81:

Lee, John R.: White, Male, Born: May 26, 1911
Father: Lee, William J. — White, Age 31, Born: Wales, Miner
Mother: Coose, Betsy — White, Age 21, Born: Iowa, 1 child born and 1 living

Lynch, Frank: Black, Male, Born: April 17, 1911
Father: Lynch, Frank — Black, Age 39, Born: Alabama, Miner
Mother: Garman, Nora — Black, Age 45, Born: Kentucky, 8 children born and 5 living

Lemonds, Chester: White, Male, Born: April 28, 1911
Father: Lemonds, Ernest R. — White, Age 31, Born: Iowa, Teamster
Mother: Cooper, Myrtle — White, Age 26, Born: Iowa, 3 children born and 3 living

Lawson, Dorthea: Black, Female, Born: December 24, 1911
Father: Lawson, Chas. — Black, Age 31, Born: Virginia
Mother: Greaver, Amanda — Black, Age 34, Born: Virginia, 2 children born and 2 living

Linger/ Lenger, George B.: White, Male, Born: June 18, 1912
Father: Linger/ Lenger, John — White, Age 43, Born: Austria, Miner
Mother: Minrsick, Mary — White, Age 29, Born: Pennsylvania, 5 children born and 5 living

Lawson, Willie: Black, Male, Born: September 9, 1912
Father: Lawson, Chas. — Black, Age 32, Born: Virginia, Miner
Mother: Grever, Amanda — Black, Age 34, Born: Virginia, 3 children born and 3 living

Long, Irene Elizabeth: White, Female, Born: May 30, 1912
Father: Long, Ed Thomas — White, Age 47, Born: Indiana, Miner
Mother: Gordon, Mary Janes — White, Age 46, Born: Illinois, 8 children born and 8 living

Lemonds, Willis: White, Male, Born: February 16, 1912
Father: Lemonds, Henry — White, Age 31, Born: Iowa, Miner
Mother: Cooper, Mary — White, Age 29, Born: Iowa, 4 children born and 3 living

PAGE 82:
Lenger, Emma: White, Female, Born: January 6, 1913
Father: Lenger, Joe — White, Age 31, Born: Austria, Miner
Mother: Mitrisin, Lizzie — White, Age 22, Born: Pennsylvania

PAGE 85:
Minaric, Geo. Washington: White, Male, Born: March 12, 1909
Father: Minaric, John — White, Age 22, Born: Austria, Miner
Mother: Zengenald, Julia — White, Age 21, Born: Austria, 1 child born and 1 living

Masters, Marjory Maxine: Race not given, Female, Illegitimate, Born: May 19, 1909
Father: No information given
Mother: Masters, Marcia Helen — White, Age 18, Born: Iowa, 1 child born and 1 living, Telephone Operator

Madison, Roy: White, Male, Born: July 4, 1909, Twin
Father: Madison, Roy — White, No age given, Born: Illinois, Miner
Mother: Madison, Francis — White, No age given, Born: Maryland, 5 children born and 2 living

Madison, Francis: White, Female, Born: July 4, 1909, Twin
Father: Madison, Roy — White, No age given, Born: Illinois, Miner
Mother: Madison, Francis — White, No age given, Born: Maryland, 5 children born and 2 living

PAGE 86:
Morgan, James: Black, Male, Born: July 1, 1910
Father: Morgan, William — Black, Age 37, Born: Virginia, Miner
Mother: Pigg, Ella — Black, Age 34, Born: Virginia, 3 children born and 3 living

Madison, Pauline: White, Female, Born: December 21, 1910
Father: Madison, Roy — White, Age 34, Born: Illinois
Mother: Tolson, Frances — White, Age 24, Born: Missouri, 6 children born and 2 living

PAGE 87:
Massey, Lenora: Black, Female, Born: November 1911
Father: Massey, Nick — Black, Age 53, Born: Virginia, Miner
Mother: Jones, Gertrude — Black, Age not given, Born: Missouri, 7 children born and 5 living

Moore, Gladys: No race given, Female, Born: 1911
Father: Moore, Bennie — No race given, Age 22, Born: West Virginia
Mother: Woods, Ollie — No race given, Age 18, Born: Iowa

Moore, Beatrice: Black, Female, Born: June 18, 1911
Father: Moore, Lloyd — Black, Age 24, Born: Virginia, Miner
Mother: Bryson, Lulu — Black, Age 22, Born: Virginia, 2 children born and 2 living

PAGE 89:
Mason, Floyd: White, Male, Born: February 29, 1912
Father: Mason, Wm. — White, Age 27, Born: England, Miner
Mother: Rice, Pansy — White, Age 25, Born: Illinois, 3 children born and 3 living

Madge, Teresa: White, Female, Born: August 11, 1912
Father: Madge, Chas. L. — White, Age 39, Born: Iowa, Miner
Mother: Dice, Frances — White, Age 31, Born: Indiana, 4 children born and 4 living

Morgan, Unnamed: Black, No gender given, Born: December 29, 1912, Stillborn
Father: Morgan, William — Black, Age 39, Born: Virginia, Miner
Mother: Pigg, Ella — Black, Age 39, Born: Virginia, 4 children born and 3 living

Manarock, Annie: White, Female, Born: October 30, 1912
Father: Manarock, Geo. — White, Age 35, Born: Austria
Mother: Siener, Annie — White, Age 29, Born: Austria, 6 children born and 6 living

Moore, John Woodrow: White, Male, Born: October 16, 1912
Father: Moore, Chas. — White, Age 31, Born: Iowa
Mother: Best, Mary A. — White, Age 30, Born: Ireland, 2 children born and 2 living

PAGE 91:

Morris, Ambrose Jr.: Black, Male, Born: February 23, 1913
Father: Morris, Ambrose Sr. — Black, Age 45, Born: Missouri, Miner
Mother: Mason, Hattie — Black, Age 45, Born: Iowa, 8 children born and 7 living

Melchion, Willis Clinton: White, Male, Born: October 25, 1913
Father: Melchion, Andy — White, Age 29, Born: Italy, Miner
Mother: Watters, Georgia — White, Age 18, Born: Iowa, 2 children born and 2 living

Mathis, Theresa: White, Male, Born: February 4, 1913
Father: Mathis, Mike — White, Age 29, Born: Illinois, Mining
Mother: No name given — White, Age 23, Born: Slavakia, 2 children born and 2 living
(This record was amended from the name Martis to the name Mathis)

Mimarsih, Margurite Leona: No race given, Female, Born: August 1, 1913
Father: Mimarsih, Jno. — No information given
Mother: Fitzgerald, Julia — No race or age given, Born: Austria

Masters, Mildred Lucille: White, Female, July 5, 1913
Father: Masters, Albert — White, Age 53, Born: Ohio, Miner
Mother: Colby, Ida — White, Age 36, Born: Not Given

Marshall, Eddy: No race given, No gender given, Born: March 24, 1913
Father: Marshall, Jas. — No race given, Age 25, Born: Kentucky, Coal Miner
Mother: Craddock, Estella — Black, Age 22, Born: Missouri, 3 children born and 2 living

PAGE 94:

Morgan, Senior Barrett: Black, Male, Born: October 12, 1914
Father: Morgan, William — Black, Age 43, Born: Virginia, Coal Miner
Mother: Pigg, Ella Synthia — Black, Age 39, Born: Virginia, 7 children born and 3 living

Martis, Mike: White, Male, Born: February 14, 1914
Father: Martis, Mike — White, Age 29, Born: Illinois, Coal Miner
Mother: Mathes, Tresa — White, Age 23, Born: Hungary

Massy, Queen Elizabeth: Black, Female, Born: May 7, 1914
Father: Massy, Nicholas — Black, Age 57, Born: Virginia, Coal Miner
Mother: Jones, Zepyh Gertrude — Black, Age 30, Born: Missouri, 8 children born and 6 living

Morris, Stephen Jr.: White, Male, Born: June 1, 1914
Father: Morris Stephen Sr. — White, Age 27, Born: Austria, Coal Miner
Mother: Bugas, Anna — White, Age 27, Born: Austria, 3 children born and 3 living

PAGE 95:

Jones, Sarah Irene: White, Female, Born: December 13, 1914
Father: Jones, John C. — White, Age 50, Born: England, Coal Miner
Mother: Spangle, Lucinda — White, Age 36, Born: Iowa, 11 children born and 9 living

PAGE 96:

Peterson, Anna Elizabeth: White, Female, Born: July 9, 1914
Father: Peterson, David — White, Age 33, Born: Sweden, Merchant
Mother: Nylander, Emma — White, Age 28, Born: Iowa, 5 children born and 5 living

Pendelton, John May: Black, Male, Born: April 14, 1914
Father: Pendleton, John — Black, Age 46, Born: Mississippi, Coal Miner
Mother: Orr, Novella — Black, Age 36, Born: Alabama, 3 children born and 3 living

Paris, Leona Rose: White, Female, Born: January 10, 1914
Father: Paris, Walter Merritt — White, Age 23, Born: Iowa, Machinist
Mother: Fisher, Bessie Elizabeth — White, Age 22, Born: Iowa, 2 children born and 3 living

Papcun, Anna: White, Female, Born: May 23, 1914
Father: Papcun, John — White, Age 24, Born: Austria, Coal Miner
Mother: Illegible, Anna — White, Age 23, Born: Pennsylvania, 5 children born and 4 living

PAGE 97:
McDonald, Leonard: Black, Male, Born: September 30, 1909
Father: McDonald, James M. — Black, Age 21, Born: Pennsylvania
Mother: Burkett, Lydia — Black, Age 20, Born: Iowa, 1 child born and 1 living

PAGE 98:
McDowell, Hubert H.: White, Male, Born: August 17, 1911
Father: McDowell, Bert — White, Age 32, Born: Iowa, Miner
Mother: Williams, Margaret — White, Age 29, Born: England, 3 children born and 2 living

McVie, Gertrude Sylvia: White, Female, Born: February 15, 1912
Father: McVie, Sam — White, Age 37, Born: Switzerland, Miner
Mother: Cavlier, Amelia — White, Age 25, Born: Belguim, 5 children born and 5 living

PAGE 99:
McBride, Wilma: White, Female, Born: January 3, 1913
Father: McBride, Claude W. — White, Age 27, Born: Kansas, Miner
Mother: Fleck, Nellie — No race given, Age 28, Born: Scotland

PAGE 100:
Nicholas, Samantha: Black, Female, Born: October 9, 1909
Father: Nicholas, James Henry — Black, Age 53, Born: Vermont, Coal Miner
Mother: Green, Cora Bertha Cecilia Clara — Black, Age 25, Born: Alabama, 2 children born and 1 living

Nelson, Edna: Black, Female, Born: May 24, 1911
Father: Nelson, Unnamed — Black, Age 23, Born: Kentucky
Mother: Clay, Madie — Black, Age 20, Born: Iowa, 2 children born and 2 living

PAGE 101:

Nicholson, Arnold: Black, Male, Born: October 9, 1911
Father: Nicholson, Henry — Black, Age 23, Born: Kentucky, Miner
Mother: Green, Bertha — Black, Age not given, Born: Alabama, 2 children born and 2 living

Nalenvanko, Lizzie: White, Female, Born: December 25, 1912
Father: Nalenvanko, John — White, Age 43, Born: Austria, Miner
Mother: Lacey, Annie — White, Age 36, Born: Austria, 7 children born and 3 living

Norberg, John Oscar Herbert: White, Male, Born: February 22, 1912
Father: Norberg, Oscar — White, Age 26, Born: Sweden, Miner
Mother: Nelson, Lydia — White, Age 22, Born: Iowa, 1 child born and 1 living

Nalevanko, Harry T.: White, Male, Born: July 3, 1913
Father: Nalevanko, Mike — White, Age 39, Born: Hungary, Farmer
Mother: Music, Irene — White, Age 35, Born: Hungary, 9 children born and 9 living

PAGE 102:

Nalevanko, Zuzi: White, Female, Born: August 4, 1913
Father: Nalevanko, Jno. — White, Age 42, Born: Hungary, Miner
Mother: Lacey, Annie — White, Age 37, Born: Austria, 8 children born and 4 living

PAGE 105:

Olson, Evelyn Josephine: White, Female, Born: May 19, 1912
Father: Olson, John B. — White, Age 34, Born: Sweden, Engineer
Mother: Larson, Anna — White, Age 37, Born: Sweden, 7 children born and 6 living

Onder, Joe: White, Male, Born: February 7, 1912
Father: Onder, , John — White, Age 39, Born: Austria
Mother: Kocerha, Barbara — White, Age 31, Born: Austria, 6 children born and 6 living

PAGE 108:

Price, Nathaniel: Black, Male, Illegitimate, Born: July 4, 1909
Father: No information given
Mother: Price, Lizzie — Black, Age 15, Born: Kentucky

Peterson, Adolpheus Reynold: White, Male, Born: June 23, 1909
Father: Peterson, David Alexis — White, Age 26, Born: Sweden, Clerk
Mother: Nylander, Emma Louise — White, Age 22, Born: Iowa, 2 children born and 2 living

Philips, Howard: Black, Male, Born: April 2, 1909
Father: Philips, William — Black, Age 24, Born: Virginia, Coal Miner
Mother: Graves, Mary — Black, Age 20, Born: West Virginia, 1 child born and 1 living

Parkey, Mauvlog Lamont: Black, Male, Born: April 12, 1909
Father: Parkey, Thomas J. — Black, Age 48, Born: Tennessee, Coal Miner
Mother: Fish, Emma — Black, Age 41, Born: Kentucky, 11 children born and 8 living

Palsik, Joseph: White, Male, Born: March 13, 1910
Father: Palsik, John — White, Age 34, Born: Austria, Miner
Mother: Thurick, Frances — White, Age 31, Born: Austria

PAGE 109:
Parker, Harry C.: Black, Male, Born: October 5, 1910
Father: Parker, Harry — Black, Age 29, Born: Ohio, Miner
Mother: Jackson, Cornelia — Black, Age 25, Born: Virginia, 4 children born and 2 living

Poe, Neoma: Black, Female, Born: May 6, 1911
Father: Poe, Green — Black, Age 35, Born: Kentucky, Miner
Mother: Marshall, Ida — Black, Age 27, Born: Virginia, 6 children born and 4 living

Parker, Harry: Black, Male, Born: October 9, 1911
Father: Parker, Harry — Black, Age 30, Born: Ohio, Miner
Mother: Jackson, Cornelia — Black, Age 29, Born: Virginia, 6 children born and 4 living

PAGE 110:
Price, Emma: White, Female, Born: December 23, 1912
Father: Price, J.H. — White, Age 38, Born: Ohio, Miner
Mother: Morgan, Sarah Ann — White, Age 37, Born: Ohio, 6 children born and 5 living

Phillips, Jennie: Black, Female, Born: February 11, 1912
Father: Phillips, Wm. — Black, Age 29, Born: Virginia, Miner
Mother: Graves, Mary — Black, Age 23, Born: West Virginia, 2 children born and 2 living

Parker, Ralph Fletcher: Black, Male, Born: June 3, 1912
Father: Parker, Harry — Black, Age 31, Born: Ohio, Miner
Mother: Jackson, Cornelia — Black, Age 30, Born: Virginia, 5 children born and 3 living

Page, Bernard Andrew: White, Male, Born: June 25, 1912
Father: Page, James Andrew — White, Age 28, Born: Iowa, Miner
Mother: Mc Roberts, Celia — White, Age 24, Born: Iowa, 2 children born and 2 living

Patterson, Alex: Black, Male, Born: November 16, 1912
Father: Patterson, Alex Sr. — Black, Male, Born: North Carolina
Mother: Tansil, Lillian — Black, Age 18, Born: Iowa, 2 children born and 2 living

Pluto, Jessie: No race listed, Female, Born: November 19, 1912
Father: Pluto, John — No race given, Age 27, Born: Austria, Miner
Mother: Platon, Blanch — No race given, Age 40, Born: Austria, 6 children born and 6 living

<h2 style="text-align:center">PAGE 114:</h2>

Lewis, Annabelle Marie: White, Female, Born: October 5, 1914
Father: Lewis, Daniel G. — White, Age 34, Born: Iowa, Miner
Mother: Wake, Mary Elizabeth — White, Age 28, Born: Iowa, 4 children born and 4 living

Lewis, Isaiah James: Black, Male, Born: March 20, 1914
Father: Lewis, Thomas Timothy — Black, Age 26, Born: Iowa, Coal Miner
Mother: Strother, Mabel Elizabeth — Black, 26, Born: Virginia, 2 children born and 2 living

<h2 style="text-align:center">PAGE 115:</h2>

Reasby, Lloyd Lewis: Black, Male, Born: July 31, 1909
Father: Reasby, William Lewis — Black, Age 22, Born: Iowa, Coal Miner
Mother: Washington, Verbana Bell — Black, Age 20, Born: Virginia, 1 child born and 1 living

<h2 style="text-align:center">PAGE 116:</h2>

Rumley, Carrol C.: Black, Age 35, Born: June 16, 1911
Father: Rumley, General — Black, Age 35, Born: Virginia, Miner
Mother: Illegible, Pearl — Black, Age 28, Born: Kansas, 5 child born and 5 living

Buxton basketball team, 1907, with mascot and game ball.

Raspatrick, Steve: White, Male, Born: October 30, 1910
Father: Raspatrick, Steve — White, Age 23, Born: Austria
Mother: Pasnihas ?, Mary — White, Age 23, Born: Austria, 1 children born and 1 living

Colhar, Mike: White, Male, Born: May 3, 1910
Father: Colhar, John — White, Age 37, Austria, Miner
Mother: Kupnas, Mary — White, Age 29, Austria, 5 children born and 5 living

Ray, Nellie M.: Black, Female, August 21, 1910
Father: Ray, Henry — Black, Age 42, Born: Kentucky, Miner
Mother: Radford, Malinda — Black, Age 37, Born: Tennessee, 6 children born and 6 living

PAGE 117:
Reasby, Verbena: Black, Female, Born: April 20, 1911
Father: Reasby, W.L. — Black, Age 24, Born: Iowa, Miner
Mother: Washington, Verbena Belle — Black, Age 22, Born: Pennsylvania, Dressmaker, 2 children born and 2 living

Reasby, Maxine: Black, Female, Born: October 27, 1911
Father: Reasby, J.N. — Black, Age 40, Born: Virginia, Miner
Mother: Kelley, Frances — Black, Age 26, Born: West Virginia, 6 children born and 4 living

PAGE 118:
Reasby, Toussaint D.: Black, Male, Born: November 11, 1912
Father: Reasby, Wm. L. — Black, Age 25, Born: Iowa, Miner
Mother: Washington, Verbena Belle — Black, Age 23, Born: Virginia, 3 children born and 3 living

Reed, Thaddens: Black, Male, Born: April 18, 1912
Father: Reed, Wm. Turner — Black, Age 45, Born: Georgia, Miner
Mother: Sander, Mary — Black, Age 30, Born: Illinois, 5 children born and 5 living

Rowlett, Cellastine Mordessa: Black, Female, Born: July 25, 1912
Father: Rowlett, John C. — Black, Age 34, Born: Illinois, Miner
Mother: Mardis, Gertrude — Black, Age 32, Born: Arkansas, 2 children born and 2 living

Rebarjak, Julia: White, Female, Born: December 13, 1912
Father: Rebarjak, John — White, Age 37, Born: Austria, Miner
Mother: Mathen, Annie — White, Age 34, Born: Austria, 5 children born and 5 living

Rhodes, Leroy: Black, Male, Born: January 30, 1912
Father: Rhodes, W.B. — Black, Age 34, Born: Virginia, Miner
Mother: Ragsdale, Mary — Black, Age 28, Born: Virginia, 5 children born and 5 living

PAGE 119:
Roberts, Lenard B.: Black, Male, Born: August 14, 1913
Father: Roberts, Geo. — Black, Age 34, Born: Iowa, Miner
Mother: Thomas, Emma — Black, Age 27, Born: Illinois

Rumley, Harvey: Black, Male, Born: April 29, 1913
Father: Rumley, General — Black, Age 31, Born: Virginia, Miner
Mother: Boyd, Pearl — Black, Age 31, Born: Kansas
(This name is spelled Rumbley in original record)

PAGE 123:
Sharp, Celestria May: Black, Female, Born: October 1, 1909
Father: Sharp, William — Black, Age 30, Born: Kentucky, Coal Miner
Mother: Black, Lucy — Black, Age 29, Born: Illinois, 4 children born and 4 living

Swinscoe, Eliza Ida: White, Female, Born: February 25, 1909
Father: Swinscoe, Henry Alfred — White, Age 36, Born: England, Coal Miner
Mother: Kline, Ella — White, Age 29, Born: Illinois, 6 children born and 6 living

Scott, Myrtle: Black, Female, Born: June 27, 1909
Father: Scott, John — Black, Age 45, Born: Virginia, Coal Miner
Mother: Smith, Emma — Black, Age 41, Born: Virginia, 4 children born and 4 living

Stewart, George: Black, Male, Born: August 27, 1909
Father: Stewart, George — Black, No age given, Born: Tennessee, Miner
Mother: Larkin, B. — Black, Age 35, Born: South Carolina, 6 children born and 4 living

Smith, Harry Thomas: White, Male, Born: November 10, 1909
Father: Smith, William — White, Age 34, Born: Iowa, Teamster
Mother: Griffiths, Anna — White, Age 24, Born: Iowa, 3 children born and 3 living

PAGE 123:

Smith, Daisy May: Black, Female, Born: August 21, 1909
Father: Smith, Daniel M. — Black, Age 36, Born: Virginia, Miner
Mother: Martin, Anna L. — Black, Age 31, Born: Virginia, 7 children born and 6 living

Spears, Rodoffice: Black, Female, Illegitimate, Born: 1909 (No other date)
Father: None Given
Mother: Spears, Ora — Black, Age 17, Born: Missouri, 1 child born and 1 living

PAGE 127:

Simms, Libbie: White, Female, Born: March 19, 1911
Father: Simms, John — White, Age 38, Born: Iowa, Miner
Mother: Luellen, Lizzie — White, Age 32, Born: Illinois, 5 children born and 5 living

Swinescoe, Henry Andrew: White, Male, Born: September 6, 1911
Father: Swinescoe, Harry — White, Age 39, Born: England, Miner
Mother: Kline, Ella — White, Age 36, Born: Illinois, 7 children born and 7 living

PAGE 128:

Santhers, Florence: Black, Female, Born: December 20, 1911
Father: Santhers, Robert — Black, Age 29, Born: Kentucky
Mother: Wenesley, Annie — Black, Age 27, Born: Kentucky, 3 children born and 3 living

PAGE 129:

Sampson, Oscar Edward: White, Male, Born: October 23, 1912
Father: Sampson, Chas. — White, Age 26, Born: Sweden, Miner
Mother: Bringman, Alta — White, Age 28, Born: Iowa, 4 children born and 4 living

PAGE 130:

Slafrosky, Steve: White, Male, Born: September 9, 1913
Father: Slafrosky, Mike — White, Age 26, Austria, Miner
Mother: Fravros, Polly — White, Age 25, Austria, 3 children born and 3 living

PAGE 131:

Smith, Rosalie: Black, Female, Born: February 28, 1913
Father: Smith, Daniel — Black, Age 47, Born: Virginia, Miner
Mother: Martin, Amy — Black, Age 35, Born: Virginia, 9 children born and 8 living

Sivak, Frank: White, Male, Born: September 22, 1913
Father: Sivak, Charles — White, Age 23, Born: Hungary, Miner
Mother: Butt, Catherine — White, Age 25, Born: Hungary

PAGE 135:
Ceglar, Steven: White, Male, Born: December 15, 1914
Father: Ceglar, Ignatz — White, Age 40, Born: Austria
Mother: Turtnik, Francis — White, Age 35, Born: Austria, 9 children born and 4 living

PAGE 136:
Sharp, Edith May: Black, Female, Born: October 31, 1914
Father: Sharp, William — Black, Age 40, Born: Kentucky, Coal Miner
Mother: Black, Lucy — Black, Age 33, Born: Tennessee, 8 children born and 6 living

PAGE 137:
Trenshaw, Steven: White, Male, Born: November 18, 1909
Father: Trenshaw, John — White, Age 32, Born: Austria
Mother: Tarkas, Rose — White, Age 23, Born: Austria, 3 children born and 3 living

Turner, George Washington: Black, Male, Born: January 22, 1909
Father: Turner, Willis Raymond — Black, Age 27, Born: Washington, Miner
Mother: Jones, Lillie Jones — Black, Age 24, Born: Iowa, 3 children born and 3 living

Tesinsky, Anna: White, Female, Born: February 28, 1909
Father: Tesinsky, Andrew — White, Age 31, Born: Austria
Mother: Rebarthick, Anna — White, Age 21, Born: Austria, 2 children born and 2 living

Thomas, Helen Isabel: White, Female, Born: September 24, 1909
Father: Thomas, David Louis — White, Age 25, Born: Iowa, Mine Engineer
Mother: Nicoll, Leah Dell — White, Age 23, Born: Nebraska, 2 children born and 2 living

PAGE 138:
Tate, Wilbert L.: Black, Male, Born: October 16, 1910
Father: Tate, Elick — Black, Age 38, Born: North Carolina, Miner
Mother: Francis, Amy — Black, Age 30, Born: North Carolina, 4 children born and 4 living

Tatin, John: White, Male, Born: July 17, 1910
Father: Tatin, Mike — White, Age 34, Born: Austria, Miner
Mother: Shatin, Mary — White, Age 34, Born: Austria, 5 children born and 5 living

Turner, Agnes: Black, Female, Born: May 24, 1910
Father: Turner, William E. — Black, Age 37, Born: Illinois, Miner
Mother: Kelnaly, Eunice — Black, Age 40, Born: Alabama, 8 children born and 8 living

Tate, Raymond F.: Black, Male, Born: June 18, 1911
Father: Tate, Ben F. — Black, Age 37, Born: Illinois, Miner
Mother: Ampey, Edna — Black, Age 30, Born: Virginia, 3 children born and 3 living

Taylor, Frank Orville: White, Male, Born: November 23, 1910
Father: Taylor, John — White, No age given, Born: Illinois
Mother: Miller, Katherine -- White, No age given, Born: Missouri

PAGE 139:
Tuego, Annie — No race given, Female, Born: July 4, 1912
Father: Tuego, John — No race or age given, Born: Italy, Miner
Mother: Tuego, Mega — No race or age given, Born: Italy, 3 children born and 3 living

Trencak, Joe: White, Male, Born: August 18, 1912
Father: Trencak, John — White, Age 35, Born: Austria, Miner
Torcak, Rosie — White, Age 26, Born: Austria, 4 children born and 4 living

Taylor, John: White, Male, Born: October 18, 1912
Father: Taylor, John H. -- White, Age 37, Born: Illinois, Fireman
Mother: Miller, Katie Ann — White, Age 28, Born: Missouri, 6 children born and 6 living   (In 1935 the name was amended to Taylor, Albert)

Toltin, Rose: White, Female, Born: May 3, 1912
Father: Toltin, Mike — White, Age 40, Born: Austria
Mother: Satan, Mary — White, Age 36, Born: Austria, 6 children born and 6 living

Thomas, Helen Madona: White, Female, Born: January 3, 1912
Father: Thomas, Harve — White, Age 35, Born: Iowa
Mother: Humphry, Bessie — White, Age 30, Born: Iowa, 4 children born and 4 living

Taylor, Gertrude Marguite: Black, Female, Born: September 12, 1912
Father: Taylor, Claud — Black, Age 24, Born: Iowa, Miner
Mother: Bates, Lucinda — Black, Age 20, Born: Iowa, 2 children born and 2 living

PAGE 140:

Tate, Lelia Mary Elizabeth: Black, Female, Born: March 5, 1912
Father: Tate, Joseph — Black, Age 35, Born: Virginia
Mother: Gibson, Lydia — Black, Age 27, Born: Iowa, 3 children born and 3 living

Traister, Lucile: White, Female, Born: 1912 (No other date given)
Father: Traister, Frank — White, Age 25, Born: Iowa
Mother: Marsh, Cora — White, Age 18, Born: Illinois, 1 child born and 1 living

Turner, Nora: Black, Female, Born: 1912 (No other date given)
Father: Turner, William — Black, Age 38, Born: Illinois, Miner
Mother: Kenley, Unis — Black, Age 42, Born: Alabama, 9 children born and 9 living

Taylor, Berthel: Black, No gender given, Born: September 23, 1913
Father: Taylor, Sloan — Black, Age 19, Born: Iowa, Miner
Mother: Mitchell, Ethel — Black, Age 18, Born: West Virginia, 1 child born and 1 living

Toran, Mary A.: Black, Female, Born: November 6, 1913
Father: Toran, Ed — Black, Age 28, Born: Virginia, Miner
Mother: Bates, Mary A.E. — Black, Age 27, Born: Iowa, 1 child born and 1 living

Tate, James: Black, Male, Born: April 12, 1913
Father: Tate, Allen — Black, Age 40, Born: Not given, Miner
Mother: Francis, Emma — Black, Age 33, Born: Not given, 5 children born and 5 living

Tursic, John Jr.: No race given, Male, Born: October 25, 1913
Father: Tursic, John — No gender or age given, Born: Yugoslavia
Mother: Rosone, Frances — No gender or age given, Born: Yugoslavia

PAGE 142:

Toler, Ethel Catherine: Black, Female, Born: September 27, 1914
Father: Toler, Wm. — Black Age 56, Born: Virginia, Miner
Mother: Doyle, Mary — Black, Age 42, Born: Virginia, 9 children born and 9 living

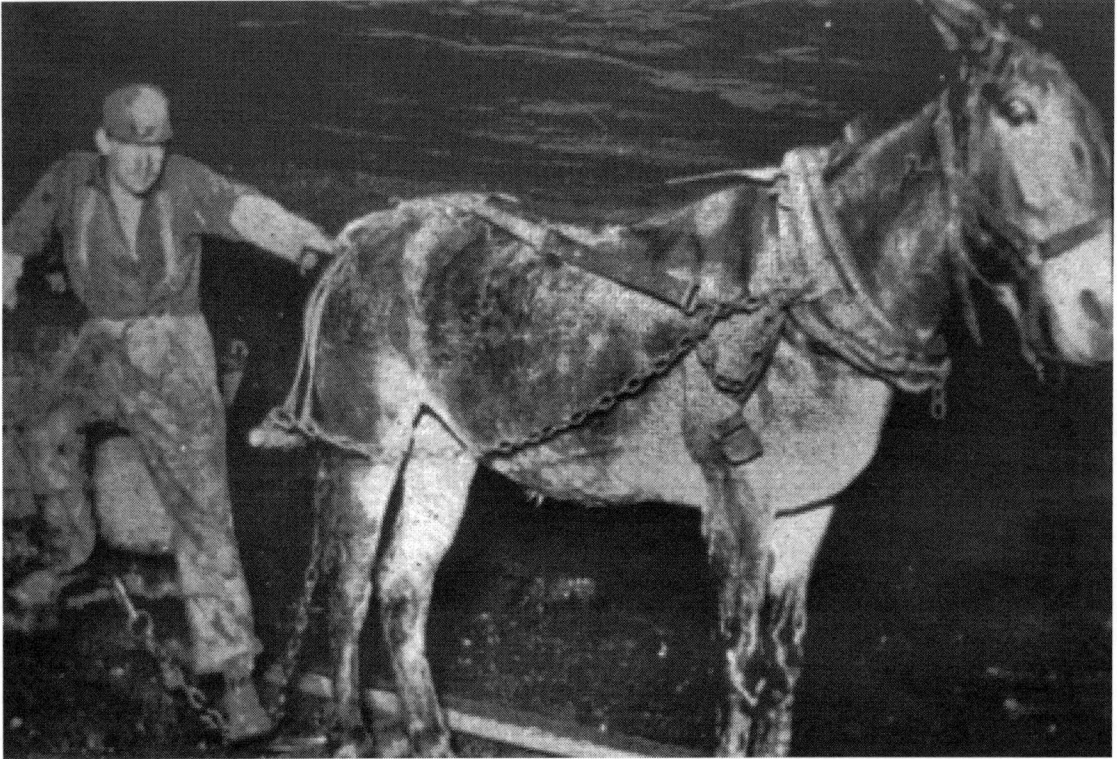

A Buxton miner works with one of the mules which were kept underground to haul coal from the mining area to the mine shaft.

Thomas, Dwight Oliver: White, Male, Born: August 13, 1914
Father: Thomas, Harvey William — White, Age 28, Born: Iowa, Miner
Mother: Humphrey, Bessie Edith — White, Age 32, Born: Iowa, 5 children born and 5 living

PAGE 146:
Vandermeulen, Helen A.: White, Female, Born: September 14, 1910
Father: Vandermeulen, Juiel — White, Age 39, Born: Belgium, Miner
Mother: Miller, Catherine — White, Age 38, Born: Germany, 4 children born and 4 living

PAGE 147:
Weaver, Maizie Frances Asolie: Black, Female, Born: October 22, 1910
Father: Weaver, Lewis — Black, Age 33, Born: Georgia
Mother: Getter, Clara — Black, Age 27, Born: Illinois, 5 children born and 5 living

Wilson, Olliver Wendell: Black, Male, Born: October 20, 1909
Father: Wilson, Luke — Black, Age 40, Born: North Carolina, Miner
Mother: Brooks, Dora — Black, Age 29, Born: Missouri, 4 children born and 4 living

Woodard, Virginia Lavurn: Black, Female, Born: January 18, 1909
Father: Woodard, Franklin Brown — Black, Age 41, Born: North Carolina, Baptist Minister
Mother: Minnis, Margaret Celeste — Black, Age 30, Born: Virginia, 2 children born and 2 living

Wilson, Paul Lawrence Dunbar: Black, Male, Born: November 25, 1909
Father: Wilson, Jacob — Black, Age 52, Born: Virginia, Miner
Mother: Logan, Lizzie — Black, Age 38, Born: Virginia, 7 children born and 2 living

Wood, Dora Nell: Black, Female, Born: May 31, 1909
Father: Wood, Bland -- Black, Age 30, Born: Virginia, Miner
Mother: Taylor, Elizabeth — Black, Age 27, Born: Missouri, 3 children born and 3 living

PAGE 148:
Wilson, Robert: Black, Male, Born: April 24, 1910
Father: Wilson, Haurice — Black, Age 22, Born: Iowa, Miner
Mother: King, Ruby — Black, Age 17, Born: Iowa, 1 child born and 1 living

Wilson, Ruth V.: White, Female, Born: May 6, 1911
Father: Wilson, Arthur — White, Age 25, Born: Iowa, Miner
Mother: Haitzer, Georgia — White, Age 23, Born: Iowa, 2 children born and 2 living

Wheels, Edmond: Black, Male, Born: December 20, 1910
Father: Wheels, James — Black, Age 56, Born: Virginia, Miner
Mother: Magus, Amanda — Black, Age 48, Born: Missouri, 11 children born and 11 living

Williams, Cordelia: Black, Female, Born: February 14, 1910
Father: Williams, Arthur — Black, Age 33, Born: Pennsylvania, Machinist
Mother: Hoggsette, Virginia — Black, Age 17, Born: Missouri, 1 child born and 1 living

Wise, Mary: Black, Female, Born: December 10, 1910
Father: Wise, Emmet — Black, Age 34, Born: Missouri, Miner
Mother: Dunning, Florence — Black, Age 37, Born: Iowa, 3 children born and 3 living

Washington, Lilia: Black, Female, Born: July 18, 1910
Father: Washington, James — Black, Age 43, Born: Virginia, Miner
Mother: Branson, Isabel — Black, Age 38, Born: Virginia, 12 children born and 11 living

Washington, Mary: Black, Female, Born: September 12, 1910
Father: Washington, William — Black, Age 38, Born: Virginia, Miner
Mother: Stiblan, Mary V. — Black, Age 35, Born: Virginia, 7 children born and 6 living

Isaacson, Evelyn D.: White, Female, Born: September 16, 1910
Father: Isaacson, Charles — White, Age 48, Born: Sweden
Mother: Fisher, Mary — White, Age not given, Born: Illinois, 8 children born and 8 living

Wilson, Adolph: Black, Male, Born: January 16, 1910
Father: Wilson, Adolph — Black, Age 24, Born: Iowa, Miner
Mother: Illegible, Ephia — Black, Age 24, Born: Missouri, 3 children born and 3 living

PAGE 149:
Watson, Catherine: White, Female, Born: September 29, 1911
Father: Watson, James — White, Age 42, Born: Scotland
Mother: Richie, Maggie — White, Age 39, Born: Scotland, 11 children born and 11 living

Wilson, Homer Henry: White, Male, Born: September 2, 1911
Father: Wilson, Harry — White, Age 35, Born: England
Mother: Silcox, Dora — White, Age 29, Born: England, 3 children born and 3 living

Weaver, Manuel: Black, Male, Born: March 2, 1911
Father: Weaver, Lewis — Black, Age 36, Born: Georgia, Miner
Mother: Getter, Clara — Black, Age 28, Born: Illinois, 6 children born and 6 living

PAGE 150:
Williams, Villeta: Black, Female, February 12, 1912
Father: Williams, John W. — Black, Age 29, Born: Virginia, Miner
Mother: Fately, Lillian — Black, Age 22, Born: Maryland, 1 child born and 1 living

Wise, Mildred: Black, Female, Born: December 25, 1912
Father: Wise, Emmet — Black, Age 36, Born: Missouri, Miner
Mother: Downey, Florence — Black, Age 28, Born: Iowa, 4 children born and 4 living

Washing, Isabell: Black, Female, Born: July 5, 1912
Father: Washing, J.H. — Black, Age 46, Born: Virginia
Mother: Granson, Isabell — Black, Age 41, Born: Virginia, 13 children born and 12 living

Watkins, Emma Ethel: White, Female, Born: June 26, 1912
Father: Watkins, Henry Wm. — White, Age 28, Born: Iowa
Mother: Foster, Lizzie — White, Age 23, Born: Iowa, 5 children born and 2 living

Wade, Silvanous Emery: Black, Male, Born: December 5, 1912
Father: Wade, Chas. — Black, Age 32, Born: Virginia, Miner
Mother: Ward, Jennie — Black, Age 20, Born: Pennsylvania, 1 child born and 1 living

Winkler, Elsie: White, Female, Born: June 1, 1912
Father: Winkler, Lucas — White, Age 30, Born: Germany, Miner
Mother: Fritz, Theris — White, Age 33, Born: Germany, 4 children born and 4 living

Wimsey, Thomas June: Black, Male, Born: November 19, 1912
Father: Wimsey, John — Black, Age 26, Born: Kentucky, Miner
Mother: Taylor, Hazel — Black, Age 19, Born: Iowa, 2 children born and 2 living

Wheels, Jas.: Black, Male, Born: March 1, 1912
Father: Wheels, Jas. — Black, Age 30, Born: North Carolina, Miner
Mother: Shade, Katie — Black, Age 20, Born: North Carolina, 2 children born and 2 living

Wilson, Robt. Wayman: Black, Male, Born: July 14, 1912
Father: Wilson, Jacob — Black, Age 53, Born: Virginia, Miner
Mother: Logan, Lizzie — Black, Age 40, Born: Virginia, 3 children born and 2 living

Wallace, Clifford Antone: Black, Male, Born: July 7, 1912
Father: Wallace, Clifford — Black, Age 26, Born: Iowa, Miner
Mother: Blakey, Lucinda — Black, Age 23, Iowa, 1 child born and 1 living

PAGE 151:
Wignal, Tommy: White, Male, Born: January 12, 1912
Father: Wignal, James — White, Age 28, Born: Iowa, Miner
Mother: Gorden, Kate — White, Age 23, Born: Iowa, 2 children born and 1 living

Wright, Lucy Marion: White, Female, Born: September 18, 1913
Father: Wright, Abraham — White, Age 54, Born: Virginia, Miner
Mother: Atwood, Mattie — White, Age 34, Born: Colorado, 6 children born and 6 living

PAGE 152:

Wilson, Vincent Charles: Black, Male, Born: July 23, 1913
Father: Wilson, Adolph — Black, Age 27, Born: Iowa, Miner
Mother: Pugh, Effie Lena — Black, Age not given, Born: Missouri

Washington, Unnamed: Black, No gender given, Stillborn, Born: March 15, 1913
Father: Washington, Wm. — Black, Age 37, Born: Virginia, Miner
Mother: Stribbling, Mary F. — Black, Age 36, Born: Virginia, 8 children born and 6 living

PAGE 154:

Wade, Charley: Black, Male, Born: February 8, 1914
Father: Wade, Charley William — Black, Age 35, Born: Virginia, Coal Miner
Mother: Ward, Jennie — Black, Age 22, Born: Virginia, 2 children born and 2 living

Whalan, Julia Elizabeth: White, Female, Born: September 16, 1914
Father: Whalan, Richard Chatman — White, Age 40, Born: Illinois, Miner
Mother: Smith, Jessie May — White, Age 26, Born: Illinois, 1 child born and 1 living

Wahl, Aner: White, Male, Born: March 21, 1914
Father: Wahl, Charles — White, Age 31, Born: Sweden, Miner
Mother: Faulkes, Goldie May — White, Age 20, Born: Iowa, 1 child born and 1 living

Watkins, Ladonna: Black, Female, Born: September 27, 1914
Father: Watkins, Sedan — Black, Age 22, Born: Iowa, Coal Miner
Mother: Watkins, Minnie — Black, Age 18, Born: Virginia, 1 child born and 1 living

Wilson, Kenneth Eugene: Black, Male, Born: January 16, 1914
Father: Wilson, Luke — Black, Age 45, Born: North Carolina, Miner
Mother: Rolls, Dora — Black, Age 36, Born: Missouri, 8 children born and 6 living

PAGE 155:
Vanarsdale, Alice: Black, Female, Born: January 5, 1914
Father: Vanarsdale, George William — Black, Age 40, Born: Kentucky, Miner
Mother: Brown, Loder — Black, Age 24, Born: Kentucky, 4 children born and 4 living

PAGE 156:
Vanarsdale, William Henry: Black, Male, Born: January 12, 1912
Father: Vanarsdale, George — Black, Age 39, Born: Kentucky, Miner
Mother: Brown, Loder — Black, Age 23, Born: Kentucky, 3 children born and 3 living

Vargasko, Mike: No race given, Male, Born: January 23, 1912
Father: Vargasko, Andy — No race given, Age 35, Born: Austria, Miner
Mother: Vosko, Mary — No race given, Age 25, Born: Austria, 2 children born and 2 living

PAGE 158:
Yusco, John: White, Male, Born: October 3, 1909
Father: Yusco, Stephen — White, Age 33, Born: Hungary, Miner
Mother: Rosepani, Susie — White, Age 26, Born: Hungary, 2 children born and 2 living

PAGE 159:
Zapuder, William: White, Male, Born: January 21, 1909
Father: Zapuder, Frank — White, Age 31, Born: Austria, Miner
Mother: Bartjancia, Johanna — White, Age 29, Born: No place given, 3 children born and 3 living

Zupusler, Mary: White, Female, Born: June 3, 1910
Father: Zupusler, Frank — White, Age 31, Born: Austria, Miner
Mother: Bantyvisick, Ginie — White, Age 31, Born: Austria, 3 children born and 3 living

Zonder, Andy: White, Male, Born: December 15, 1912
Father: Zonder, Chas. — White, Age 40, Born: Austria
Mother: Adams, Anna — White, Age 34, Born: Austria, 6 children born and 6 living

Above: Swedish Lutheran Church, Buxton, Iowa. The building survived the dismantling of the town of Buxton; it burned to the ground on December 20, 1954.

Left: The bell of the Swedish Lutheran Church, on display at the Monroe County Historical Society museum. At right is a closer view of the lettering on the bell.

Interior of the Swedish Lutheran Church, Buxton, Iowa. The altar painting was created
by the Swedish-American painter Sandzen. The painting was removed before the
church building was destroyed by fire and is on display
at the Monroe County Historical Society museum in Albia, Iowa.

Monroe County, Iowa Birth Book 4
1915 to 1917

Information Recorded:
This county record book of births includes child's name, race, gender, birth date, father's name, race, age, place born, occupation, mother's name, race, age, birth place, number of children born and number of children still living. The page number of the record book where the birth is recorded has been included for the convenience of researchers.

PAGE 1:
Anderson, Beatrice: Black, Female, Born: May 28, 1915
Father: Anderson, John — Black, Age 39, Born: Virginia, Coal Miner
Mother: Garnett, Ruth — Black, Age 28, Born: Iowa, 2 children born and 2 living

Antol, Emma: White, Female, Born: August 12, 1915
Father: Antol, George — No race given, Age 43, Born: Pennsylvania
Mother: Kapka, Mary — White, Age 37, Born: None given

PAGE 2:
Anderson, Norman Ballad: Black, Male, Born: December 25, 1917
Father: Anderson, John — Black, Age 42, Born: Virginia, Miner
Mother: Garnett, Ruth — Black, Age 30, Born: Iowa, 4 children born and 3 living

PAGE 7:
Brown, Carey Isabelle: No race given, Female, Born: April 19, 1915
Father: Brown, Jack — No race given, Age 20, Born: Iowa, Miner
Mother: Downs, Orpha — No race given, Age 20, Born: Iowa, 1 child born and 1 living

PAGE 8:
Blackstone, Clara Georgana: White, Female, Born: January 28, 1915
Father: Blackstone, Chas.L. — White, Age 43, Born: Iowa, Coal Miner
Mother: Deith, Francis — White, Age 33, Born: Indiana, 5 children born and 5 living

Butcher, Ruth: White, Female, Born: February 23, 1915
Father: Butcher, Romeo — White, Age 28, Born: West Virginia, Miner
Mother: Chambers, Ethel — White, Age 21, Born: Iowa, 2 children born and 2 living

PAGE 9:

Brewer, Gordan Hale: White, Male, Born: August 12, 1916
Father: Brewer Herbert B. — White, Age 37, Born: Iowa, Salesman
Mother: Page, Pearl — White, Age 27, Born: Iowa

Brinker, Joseph: Black, Male, Illegitimate, Born: April 28, 1916
Father: Garrett, Joseph — Black, Age 39, Born: Kansas, Miner
Mother: Brinker, Dorsey — Black, Age 38, Born: Iowa, 1 child born and 1 living

Baker, Opal Delorise: White, Female, October 15, 1916
Father: Baker, Fred — White, Age 23, Born: Iowa
Mother: Bolton, Maggie — White, Age 22, Born: Iowa, 2 children born and 2 living

Barrett, Eugene: White, Male, Born: June 12, 1916
Father: Barrett, Ed — White, Age 28, Born: Iowa, Teamster
Mother: Hereha, Anna — White, Age 23, Born: Iowa, 2 children born and 2 living

Brewer, Chas.: Black, Male, Born: September 2, 1916
Father: Brewer, Chas. — Black, Age 28, Born: Iowa, Miner
Mother: Mair, Adda — Black, Age 26, Born: Virginia, 2 children born and 2 living

Baxter, Annabeth: White, Female, No date given
Father: Baxter, Merl — White, Age 26, Born: Iowa, Clerk
Mother: Massenger, Lulu — White, Age 25, Born: Colorado, 3 children born and 3 living

PAGE 10:

Brooks, Evelyn Flora: Black, Female, Born: November 11, 1916
Father: Brooks, George — Black, Age 46, Born: Virginia
Mother: Roland, Lulu — Black, No age given, Born: Tennessee, ? Children born and 9 living

PAGE 11:

Barton, Rolland Donald: Black, Male, Born: November 8, 1917
Father: Barton, James — Black, Age 33, Born: Tennessee, Miner
Mother: Massey, Luella — Black, Age 23, Born: Colorado, 3 children born and 3 living

Belonsky, Annie: No race given, Female, Born: December 8, 1917
Father: Belonsky, John — No race given, Age 34, Born: Austria, Miner
Mother: Machanas, Lizzie — No race given, Age 28, Born: Austria, 4 children born and 4 living

Bregar, Albert Joseph: White, Male, Born: July 11, 1917
Father: Bregar, Frank — White, No age given, Born: Austria
Mother: Pestotnik, Annie — White, No age given, Born: Austria

PAGE 27:
Clark, Flossie: Black, Female, Illegitimate, Born: August 19, 1915
Father: None given
Mother: Clark, Danilee — Black, Age 19, Born: Tennessee, 1 child borm and 1 living

Croft, Everett: White, Male, Born: June 30, 1915
Father: Croft, Ben — White, Age 27, Born: Iowa, Teamster
Mother: Pierce, Etta — White, Age 25, Born: Iowa, 3 children born and 2 living

Carlson, Opal: White, Female, Born: August 13, 1915
Father: Carlson, Gus — White, Age 39, Born: Sweden, Coal Miner
Mother: Larson, Mary — White, Age 34, Born: Iowa, 5 children born and 5 living

Coghlan, Adrian: White, Male, Born: November 5, 1915
Father: Coghlan, Roy — White, Age 19, Born: Iowa, Coal Miner
Mother: Harris, Hilda — White, Age 17, Born: Wales

PAGE 29:
Cooper, Everitt: White, Male, Born: December 24, 1916
Father: Cooper, F.Z. — White, Age 22, Born: Iowa, Miner
Mother: Cottrell, Gladys — White, Age 20, Born: Iowa

Codell, Chester: White, Male, Born: January 21, 1917
Father: Codell, Gus — White, Age 29, Born: Iowa, Miner
Mother: Anderson, Gertie — White, Age 27, Born: Iowa, ? Children born and 2 living

PAGE 30:
Clayborne, Wearmeater: Black, Female, Born: February 5, 1917
Father: Clayborne, Alfred — Black, Age 32, Born: Iowa, Miner
Mother: Nicholas, Allie — Black, Age 26, Iowa, 4 children born and 4 living
(This record states she was born on a Boone Co., Iowa farm.)

Carr, George: Black, Male, Born: August 24, 1917
Father: Carr, George — Black, Age 32, Born: Iowa, Miner
Mother: Robinson, Mary — Black, Age 26, Born: Iowa, 5 children born and 4 living

Carter, Russell: Black, Male, Born: May 28, 1917
Father: Carter, Clinton — Black, Age 26, Born: Iowa, Miner
Mother: Parkey, Ida — Black, Age 21, Born: Virginia, 1 child born and 1 living

Cadell, Marvin Chester: White, Male, Born: January 21, 1917
Father: Cadell, Gus — White, Age 30, Born: Iowa, Miner
Mother: Anderson, Gertie — White, Age 27, Born: Iowa, 2 children born and 2 living

PAGE 38:
Davis, Lenard: Black, Male, Born: June 13, 1915
Father: Davis, Ernest — Black, Age 18, Born: Not given, Coal Miner
Mother: Roach, Edna — Black, Age 17, Born: Iowa, 1 child born and 1 living

Denchok, Helen: White, Female, Born: June 12, 1915
Father: Denchok, Jno. — White, Age 30, Born: Whiteburg
Mother: Denchok, Anna — White, Age 22, Born: Austria, 2 children born and 2 living

Denin, Rachel Elsie: White, Female, Born: April 2, 1915
Father: Denin, Lester — White, Age 28, Born: Iowa
Mother: Tyrrel, Bessie — White, Age 24, Born: Iowa, 1 child born and 1 child living

PAGE 48:
Engstrom, Barney: White, Male, Born: August 20, 1915
Father: Engstrom, Gus — White, Age 48, Born: Not given, Coal Miner
Mother: Larson, Rena — White, Age 40, Born: Sweden, 10 children born and 10 living

Ewing, Lenard: Black, Male, Illegitimate, Born: July 16, 1916
Father: None given
Mother: Ewing, Inez -- Black, Age 16, Born: Iowa

Ewings, Lean: Black, Male, Illegitimate, Born: September 10, 1917, Stillborn
Father: Seavers, Cecil — Black, Age 18, Born: Not given, Miner
Mother: Ewings, Enice — Black, Age 14, Born: Iowa, 1 child born and 0 living

Page 55:
Fesko, Mike: No race given, Male, Born: April 7, 1917
Father: Fesko, George — No race given, Age 33, Born: Austria, Miner
Mother: Slatsky, Annie — No race given, Age 27, Born: Pennsylvania, 6 children born and 6 living

Page 64:
Gasper, George: White, Male, April 7, 1917
Father: Gasper, John — White, Age 39, Born: Austria, Miner
Mother: Vargo, Lizzie — White, Age 40, Born: Austria, 4 children born and 4 living

Gilbert, Eva: White, Female, Born: June 27, 1915
Father: Gilbert, Geo. — White, Age 45, Born: Iowa
Mother: Petrovch, Matilda — White, Age 40, Born: Not given, 4 children born and 4 living

Page 65:
Gibbons, William Edward Jr.: Black, Male, Born: July 21, 1917
Father: Gibbons, Wm. E. -- Black, Age 25, Born: Iowa, Miner
Mother: Gordan, Nettie — Black, Age 18, Born: Illinois, 1 child born and 0 living

Goodwin, James Edward: White, Male, Born: June 28, 1917
Father: Goodwin, Unnamed — White, Age 33, Born: Iowa, Miner
Mother: Nickles, Osabell — White, Age 25, Born: Iowa, 3 children born and 3 living

Graves, Joseph: No race given, Male, Born: May 4, 1916
Father: Graves, Lee — No race or age given, Born: West Virginia
Mother: Cole, Helen — No race or age given, Born: West Virginia
(This birth was not recorded until January 30, 1942)

Page 76:
Hall, Sylvester: Black, Male, Illegitimate, Born: March 31, 1915
Father: None given
Mother: Bryant, Salie — Black, Age 31, Born: Iowa, 1 children born and 1 living

Hudok, Joe: White, Male, Born: April 3, 1916
Father: Hudok, Steve — White, Age 24, Born: Austria, Miner
Mother: Chunko, Tressa — White, Age 23, Born: Austria, ? Children born and 2 living

Hunt, Russell: White, Male, Born: October 12, 1916
Father: Hunt, Henry — White, Age 23, Born: Colorado, Miner
Mother: Raymond, Lydia — White, Age 21, Born: Colorado, ? Children born and 1 living

PAGE 77:
Howard, Margarie: Black, Female, Born: March 15, 1917
Father: Howard, Herman C. — Black, Age 24, Born: Kentucky, Miner
Mother: Garnett, Bertha — Black, Age 23, Born: Iowa, 1 child born and 1 living

Hogglund, Albert Marvin: White, Male, Born: March 27, 1917
Father: Hogglund, Albert — White, Age 28, Born: Iowa, Clerk
Mother: Bloomgren, Bettie — White, Age 24, Born: Iowa, 3 children born and 3 living

PAGE 95:
Jones, Marcellus: Black, Gender not given, Born: July 20, 1915
Father: Jones, Ed — Black, Age 45, Born: Virginia, Coal Miner
Mother: Wilson, Daisy — Black, Age 36, Born: Virginia, 5 children born and 5 living

Jenkins, Doris Mary Lee: Black, Female, Born: April 1, 1915
Father: Jenkins, Samuel James — Black, Age 38, Born: Missouri
Mother: Wilson, Flora Lee — Black, Age 17, Born: Illinois, 1 child born and 1 living

Jones, Louise: Black, Female, Born: November 22, 1915
Father: Jones, Chas. P. — Black, Age 33, Born: Virginia, Coal Miner
Mother: Ellis, Lulu — Black, Age 30, Born: Iowa, 5 children born and 5 living

Jewett, Catherine: Black, Female, Born: No date given
Father: Jewett, Wm. — Black, Age 31, Born: Virginia, Coal Miner
Mother: Amphy, Margurite — Black, Age 25, Born: Iowa, 1 child born and 1 living

Johnson, Margaret Eleanor: White, Female, Born: September 13, 1915
Father: Johnson, Ludwig — White, Age 32, Born: Sweden, Coal Miner
Mother: Carlson, Sigrid — White, Age 22, Born: Minnesota, 2 children born and 2 living

Jones, Adolph Reuben: Black, Male, Born: March 11, 1915
Father: Jones, Adolph — Black, Age 22, Born: Iowa
Mother: Brown, Alice — Black, Age 21, Born: Iowa, 2 children born and 1 living

Jones, Albert Alvin: White, Male, Born: October 31, 1916 (Twin)
Father: Jones, John C. — White, Age 52, Born: England, Miner
Mother: Spangle, Vicindy — White, Age 39, Born: Iowa, 13 children born and 11 living

Jones, Alberta Alma: White, Female, Born: October 31, 1916 (Twin)
Father: Jones, John C. — White, Age 52, Born: England, Miner
Mother: Spangle, Vicindy — White, Age 39, Born: Iowa, 13 children and 11 living

Jenkins, Samuel B.: No race given, Male, Born: September 14, 1916
Father: Jenkins, Samuel — No race given, Age 39, Born: Illinois, Miner
Mother: Wilson, Flora — No race given, Age 18, Born: Illinois, 2 children born and 2 living

Johnson, Dwight: White, Male, Born: August 24, 1916
Father: Johnson, Dave — White, Age 26, Born: Iowa
Mother: Pollock, Jennie — White, Age 23, Born: Ohio, ? Children born and 2 living

PAGE 102:
Kubasek, Joseph Martin: White, Male, Born: August 15, 1917
Father: Kubasek, Steve — White, Age 30, Born: Austria, Mining
Mother: Durbala, Anna — White, Age 30, Born: Austria, 3 children born and 2 living

PAGE 109:
Lenger, Joseph Martin: White, Male, Born: May 5, 1915
Father: Lenger, Joseph — White, Age 34, Born: Austria, Coal Miner
Mother: Mitrisin, Lizzie — White, Age 25, Born: Pennsylvania, 3 children born and 3 living

PAGE 110:
Lash, Elsie May: White, Female, Illegitimate, Born: April 20, 1916
Father: None given
Mother: Lash, Nellie — White, Age 16, Born: Missouri, 1 child born and 1 living

Page 128:

Miller, Earl: Black, Male, Born: May 10, 1915
Father: Miller, Harry — Black, Age 44, Born: Tennessee, Coal Miner
Mother: Payne, Lucy — Black, Age 36, Born: Virginia, 9 children born and 8 living

Morris, Guy Edmund: Black, Male, Born: May 31, 1916
Father: Morris, Guy Edmund — Black, Age 28, Born: Marion Co., Iowa, Miner
Mother: Brooks, Lulah — Black, Age 25, Born: Mahaska Co., Iowa, 1 child born and 1 living

Page 129:

Miller, Minnie: Black, Female, Born: May 5, 1916
Father: Miller, John T. — Black, Age 46, Born: Virginia, Miner
Mother: Micheal, Rosie — Black, Age 22, Born: North Carolina, 1 child born and 1 living

Miller, Bernice: Black, Female, Born: June 7, 1917
Father: Miller, Josh — Black, Age 30, Born: Alabama, Miner
Mother: Miller, Magnolia — No race or age given, Born: Iowa, 1 child born and 1 living

Massey, Franklin Ralph: Black, Male, Born: November 10, 1916
Father: Massey, Mick — Black, Age 57, Born: Virginia, Miner
Mother: Johns, Jephra — Black, Age 32, Born: Missouri, ? Children born and 6 living

Miles, Dorothy: Black, Female, Born: October 25, 1916
Father: Miles, Clifton — Black, Age 22, Born: Iowa, Miner
Mother: Johnson, Minta — Black, Age 18, Born: Iowa, ? Children born and 1 living

Page 130:

Mays, Marjorie: Black, Female, Born: 1917 (No other dates given)
Father: Mays, Leonard — Black, Age 23, Born: Virginia, Miner
Mother: Washington, Anna — Black, Age 23, Born: Virginia

Page 142:

McFarland, Paul: White, Male, Born: March 17, 1915
Father: McFarland, Floyd — White, Age 23, Born: Nebraska
Mother: Belzer, Bessie — White, Age 19, Born: Missouri, 3 children born and 2 living

PAGE 146:

Nickles, Thomas: White, Male, Born: May 28, 1916
Father: Mickles, Wm. — White, Age 29, Born: England, Miner
Mother: Goodwin, Loretta — White, Age 31, Born: Iowa, ? Children born and 2 living

PAGE 158:

Pazel, Helen: White, Female, Born: June 2, 1915
Father: Pazel, Steve — White, Age 34, Born: Austria
Mother: Bogus, Anna — White, Age 26, Born: Austria, 2 children born and 2 living

Phillips, John William: Black, Male, No birth date given
Father: Phillips, Wm. — Black, Age 30, Born: None given
Mother: Graves, Mary — Black, Age 25, Born: West Virginia, 3 children born and 3 living

Buxton Wonders baseball team, date not known.

Patterson, Willis Elwood: White, Male, Born: July 1, 1915
Father: Patterson, Stewart — White, Age 23, Born: Iowa, Coal Miner
Mother: Thomas, Irene — White, Age 21, Born: Iowa, 1 child born and 1 living

PAGE 159:
Prothero, Lillian: White, Female, Born: February 21, 1916
Father: Prothero, Geo. — White, Age 39, Born: Illinois
Mother: Isaacon, Signa — White, Age 24, Born: Mahaska Co., Iowa, 1 child born and 1 living

Pierce, Richard: White, Male, Born: October 4, 1916
Father: Pierce, Earl — White, Age 27, Born: Iowa, Coal Miner
Mother: Humphrey, Ida — White, Age 24, Born: Iowa. ? Children born and 3 living

Pierce, Lovaugh: White, Male, Born: September 2, 1916
Father: Pierce, Ernest — White, Age 22, Born: Iowa, Miner
Mother: Schwartz, Blanch — White, Age 20, Born: Austria, ? Children born and 1 living

PAGE 160:
Peterson, John Herland: White, Male, Born: October 9, 1917
Father: Peterson, Edward — White, Age 32, Born: Iowa, Miner
Mother: Berkquist, Eva — White, Age 31, Born: Iowa, 4 children born and 3 living

PAGE 166:
Reasby, Nathan: Black, Male, Born: September 8, 1915
Father: Reasby, John N. — Black, Age 43, Born: Virginia, Coal Miner
Mother: Kelly, Frances — Black, Age 30, Born: West Virginia, 8 child born and 5 living

Rumbly, Margurite: Black, Female, Born: September 2, 1915
Father: Rumbly, General — Black, Age 40, Born: Virginia, Coal Miner
Mother: Boyd, Pearl — Black, Age 33, Born: Kansas, 7 children born and 7 living

PAGE 167:
Reasby, Cora: Black, Female, Born: April 20, 1916/1917
Father: Reasby, Hearnden — Black, Age 34, Born: Iowa
Mother: Curry, Massey — Black, Age 32, Born: Iowa, ? Children born and 4 living

Roland, Lee W.: White, Male, Born: February 21, 1917
Father: Roland, Oscar J. — White, Age 28, Born: Belgium, Clerk
Mother: Lee, Sadie — White, Age 25, Born: Colorado, 1 child born and 1 living

PAGE 178:
Sulentich, Frank: White, Male, Born: July 5, 1915
Father: Sulentich, John — White, Age 27, Born: Austria, Miner
Mother: Budock, Kathryn — White, Age 22, Born: Austria, 1 child born and 1 living

PAGE 179:
Smith, Edward Taylor: Black, Male, Born: March 5, 1915
Father: Smith, Clarence — Black, Age 23, Born: Kentucky
Mother: Cronk, Harriett — Black, Age 21, Born: Iowa, 1 child born and 1 living

Sivak, Wilhemina: White, Female, Born: June 19, 1915
Father: Sivak, Chas. — White, Age 26, Born: Austria, Coal Miner
Mother: Behanec, Catherine — White, Age 26, Born: Austria, 4 children born and 4 living

Schoolen, Earl Patrick: No race given, Male, Born: June 1, 1915
Father: Schoolen, Pat — No race given, Age 29, Born: Iowa, Coal Miner
Mother: Bringman, Blanche — No race given, Age 25, Born: Iowa, 2 children born and 2 living

PAGE 182:
Steinbach, Wilhelmina Elizabeth: White, Female, Born: March 31, 1917
Father: Steinbach, Frank — White, Age 29, Born: Illinois, Mining
Mother: Evans, Margaret — White, Age 21, Born: England, 1 child born and 1 living

Smith, Dorothy: Black, Female, Born: July 15, 1917
Father: Smith, Clarence — Black, Age 25, Born: Kentucky
Mother: Crank, Harriett J. — Black, Age 24, Born: Iowa, 2 children born and 2 living

PAGE 198:
Tate, Mildred: Black, Female, Born: October 8, 1915
Father: Tate, Alex — Black, Age 44, Born: North Carolina, Coal Miner
Mother: Francis, Emma — Black, Age 35, Born: North Carolina, 6 children born and 6 living

Thomas, Arthur Melvin: Black, Male, Born: 1915 (No other dates given)
Father: Thomas, Calvin — Black, Age 47, Born: Alabama, Coal Miner
Mother: Bell, Lurana — Black, Age 38, Born: Missouri, 6 children born and 5 living

PAGE 199:

Turner, Beatrice Alice: Black, Female, Born: January 25, 1915
Father: Turner, David — Black, Age 22, Born: Illinois, Coal Miner
Mother: Doyle, Hattie — Black, Age 21, Born: Virginia

Taylor, Sloan: Black, Male, Born: February 2, 1916
Father: Taylor, Sloan Sr. — Black, Age 22, Born: Iowa, Miner
Mother: Thomas, Ethel — Black, Age 22, Born: Virginia, 1 child born and 1 living

Thomas, James Edward: Black, Male, Born: August 9, 1917
Father: Thomas, Calvin — Black, Age 49, Born: Alabama, Miner
Mother: Bell, Lurena — Black, Age 42, Born: Missouri, 12 children born and 6 living

PAGE 213:

Washington, Rosetta Teressa: Black, Female, Born: October 29, 1915
Father: Washington, Wm. — Black, Age 46, Born: Virginia. Miner
Mother: Stribbling, Mary Frances — Black, Age 39, Born: Virginia, 7 children born and 7 living

Wade, James Henry: Black, Male, Born: October 23, 1915
Father: Wade, Chas. — Black, Age 34, Born: Virginia, Miner
Mother: Ward, Jennie — Black, Age 23, Born: Virginia, 3 children born and 3 living

Ward, Lessie: Black, Female, Born: April 30, 1915
Father: Ward, Harris — Black, Age 27, Born: Virginia, Miner
Mother: Fox, Golden — Black, Age 19, Born: Kentucky, 1 child born and 1 living

Williams, Margurite: Black, Female, Born: July 10, 1915
Father: Williams, Paris — Black, Age 44, Born: Ohio, Miner
Mother: Thomas, Bessie — Black, Age 25, Born: Virginia

Wahl, Mary Margurite: White, Female, Born: October 10, 1915
Father: Wahl, Chas. — White, Age 33, Born: Not given
Mother: Foulks, Goldia — White, Age 20, Born: Iowa, 2 children born and 2 living

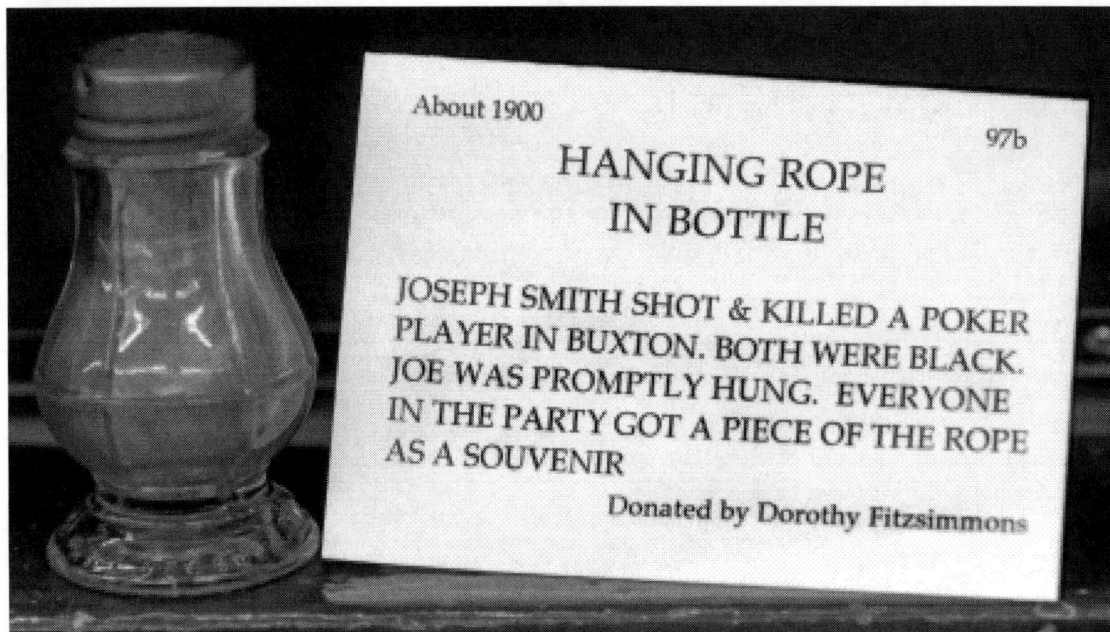

"Souvenir" piece of a rope said to have been used in a hanging in Buxton, on display at the Monroe County Historical Society museum.

PAGE 214:

Williams, Blanch: Black, Female, Born: July 18, 1916
Father: Williams, Paris — Black, Age 46, Born: Ohio, Miner
Mother: Thomas, Bessie — Black, Age 27, Born: Virginia, 4 children born and 4 living

Washington, Rosetta: No information given
Father: Washington, Wm. — Black, Age 46, Born: Virginia, Miner
Mother: Scribbling, Mary — Black, Age 39, Born: Virginia, 8 children born and 8 living

Wheels, Wm.: Black, Male, Born: April 4, 1916
Father: Wheels, Wm. — Black, Age 28, Born: Iowa, Miner
Mother: Doyal, Maddie — Black, Age 20, Born: Virginia, ? Children born and 1 living

Monroe Co., Iowa Birth Book 5
1918 to 1929

Information Recorded:
This county record book of births includes child's name, gender, date of birth, father's name, mother's name. The page number of the record book where the birth is recorded has been included for the convenience of researchers.

PAGE 1:
Allen, Phyllis Marion: Female, Born: January 13, 1920, Father's Name: Allen, Gustavis — Mother's Name: Bloom, Della

PAGE 2:
Ampey, Marvin David: Male, Born: February 24, 1921, Father's Name: Ampey, David — Mother's Name: Ampey, Arminta

PAGE 7:
Bievas, [Unreadable]: Female, Born: May 7, 1918, Father's Name: Bievas, John — Mother's Name: Holza, Anna

Blaney, John William: Male, Born: June 8, 1918, Father's Name: Blaney, John W. — Mother's Name: Watkins, Lizzie

Bloomgren, Cal Ralph: Male, Born: August 14, 1918, Father's Name: Bloomgren, Emanuel — Mother's Name: Larson, Matilda

PAGE 8:
Baker, Paul Franklin: Male, Born: November 7, 1918, Father's Name: Baker, Paul — Mother's Name: Garnett, Lizzie

Butcher, Nina Elinor: Female, Born: January 29, 1919, Father's Name: Butcher, William Delmar — Mother's Name: Richmond, Della Dilia

PAGE 10:

Bourland, Celine Adeline: Female, Born: January 7, 1921, Father's Name: Bourland, Theodore Jr. — Mother's Name: Martin, Pauline

Bates, Unnamed: Male, Born: April 21, 1921 (Stillborn), Father's Name: Bates, Charles B. — Mother's Name: Clayborne, Maime

PAGE 12:

Blomgren, Carl Virgil: Male, Born: July 20, 1924, Father's Name: Blomgren, Carl Wm. — Mother's Name: Olson, Edna Victor

PAGE 15:

Bell, Donald Irvin: Male, Born: June 12, 1926, Father's Name: Bell, Emmett — Mother's Name: Lewis, Agnes Thelma

PAGE 27:

Coop, Elma Caresta: Female, Born: April 13, 1918, Father's Name: Coop, Robert T. — Mother's Name: Nardby, Florence H.

PAGE 28:

Carter, William Edward: Male, Born: November 18, 1918, Father's Name: Carter, Wm Edward — Mother's Name: Carpenter, Susie

Coleman, Carmelita Lucile Sach: Female, Born: April 10, 1919, Father's Name: Coleman, Fred — Mother's Name: Sach, Nellie

Clay, Everet Arthur: Male, Born: May 31, 1919, Father's Name: Clay, Everet — Mother's Name: Mills, Minnie

Carter, Doris Winnifred: Female, Born: June 10, 1919, Father's Name: Carter, Clinton — Mother's Name: Parkey, Ida

Carter, Marjorie: Female, Born: July 17, 1919, Father's Name: Carter, Dr. E.A. — Mother's Name: Warren, Rose Etta

Calvert, Viola Alice: Female, Born: July 23, 1919, Father's Name: Calvert, Edward — Mother's Name: Church, Viola Alice

PAGE 29:
Church, Fredie Eugene: Male, Born: October 17, 1919, Father's Name: Church, Fred — Mother's Name: Weeks, Mary

PAGE 31:
Clair, Clarence Edward: Male, Born: February 25, 1921, Father's Name: Clair, Thomas Leslie — Mother's Name: Cooper, Nettie Jane

Carter, Louise: Female, Born: January 9, 1921, Father's Name: Carter Eddie — Mother's Name: Carter, Susie

Carlson, Elsie Ethel: Female, Born: June 2, 1921, Father's Name: Carlson, Ernest — Mother's Name: Anderson, Lizzie May

PAGE 32:
Church, Roy Edward: Male, Born: June 11, 1922, Father's Name: Church, Fred Wesley — Mother's Name: Weeks, Mary Lucille

PAGE 39:
Dyke, Unnamed: No gender given, Born: April 12, 1918, Father's Name: Dyke, Aaron — Mother's Name: Preveer, Ruby Mae

PAGE 50:
Ewing, Magnolia: Female, Born: January 15, 1921, Father's Name: Carr, Ernest — Mother's Name: Ewing, S.

PAGE 57:
Ferguson, Margaret Lee: Female, Born: December 29, 1920, Father's Name: Ferguson, Walter — Mother's Name: Ferguson, Valley

PAGE 67:
Glasford, Lewis: Male, Born: January 14, 1921, Father's Name: Glasford, Basil Ernest — Mother's Name: Martin, Ella May

Glasford, Louise: Female, Born: January 14, 1921, Father's Name: Glasford, Basil Ernest — Mother's Name: Martin, Ella May

Adolphus Glenn
My first husband

Written by Muggie Belve Adams

Buxton resident Adolphus Glenn

PAGE 68:

Gardner, Mildred Isabell: Female, Born: February 28, 1922, Father's Name: Gardner, Chas. F. — Mother's Name: Taylor, Lovina J.

PAGE 77:

Hunt, Bernard: Male, Born: April 20, 1918, Father's Name: Hunt, Wm. — Mother's Name: McGilvrey, Ruth

Haifley, Virgil Eugene: Male, Born: December 17, 1918, Father's Name: Haifley, Ira Wm. — Mother's Name: Miller, Mary Elnora

PAGE 79:

Hill, Susie Leola: Female, Born: November 6, 1920, Father's Name: Hill, Frank — Mother's Name: Hill, Ollie

Harris, Thomas John: Male, Born: February 19, 1921, Father's Name: Harris, Herbert — Mother's Name: Cooper, Bessie Edith

Hill, Clarence: Male, Born: February 18, 1921, Father's Name: Hill, Chas. Lee — Mother's Name: Hill, Laura Haines

PAGE 81:

Hoover, Roy Emery: Male, Born: June 19, 1923, Father's Name: Hoover, Joseph E. — Mother's Name: McMillion, Lela

PAGE 96:

Jenkins, Mildred Hester: Female, Born: March 29, 1918, Father's Name: Jenkins, Samuel James — Mother's Name: Wilson, Flora Lee

PAGE 100:

Jones, Shirley: Female, Born: April 19, 1924, Father's Name: Jones, Ed Jr. — Mother's Name: Jones, Gladys Smith

PAGE 103:

Klobnak, George: Male, Born: April 29, 1921, Father's Name: Klobnak, Andrew — Mother's Name: Mata, Elizabeth

PAGE 110:

Lee, Esther Louise: Female, Born: January 14, 1918, Father's Name: Lee, Wm. J. — Mother's Name: Coop, Betsy

PAGE 111:

Luke, John Andrew: Male, Born: April 12, 1921, Father's Name: Luke, John Elvin — Mother's Name: Erickson, Doris

PAGE 120:

Montjoy, Mae Alena: Female, Born: May 3, 1918, Father's Name: Montjoy, Sam — Mother's Name: Mardis, Louise

Mayer, Ruth Elouise: Female, Born: June 26, 1918, Father's Name: Mayer, Lamon George — Mother's Name: Wallace, Lillian

Merrill, Leora Mildred: Female, Born: October 19, 1918, Father's Name: Merrill, Howard — Mother's Name: Spann, Viva

PAGE 121:

Massey, Erma May: Female, Born: April 19, 1919, Father's Name: Massey, Nick — Mother's Name: Jones, Jeffrie Gertrude

PAGE 122:

Morve, Hugh Morgan: Male, Born: January 22, 1921, Father's Name: Morve, Samuel Thomas — Mother's Name: Jones, Margaret Mary

PAGE 142:

Norberg, Robert Melvin: Male, Born: December 30, 1918, Father's Name: Norberg, Oscar — Mother's Name: Nelson, Alida

Nichols, Elias Howard: Male, Born: May 13, 1921, Father's Name: Nichols, Henry — Mother's Name: Lewis, Elizabeth

PAGE 148:

Ousley, [Unreadable]: Female, Born: June 8, 1918, Father's Name: Ousley, Herschell — Mother's Name: Lee, Lillian

Owen, Johnny: Male, Born: December 17, 1920, Father's Name: Owen, Oscar — Mother's Name: Owen, Georgia

PAGE 154:

Provis, Vergina Agnes: Female, Born: April 24, 1918, Father's Name: Provis, William Eugene — Mother's Name: Hreha, Emma P.

Pollock, Bernice Eveland: Female, Born: October 23, 1918, Father's Name: Pollock, John — Mother's Name: Collins, Blanche

PAGE 155:

Pino, Rachel Lucia: Female, Born: January 9, 1921, Father's Name: Pino, Angelo — Mother's Name: Ravers, Rosa

PAGE 163:

Rumley, Joseph: Male, Born: May 18, 1918, Father's Name: Rumley, General — Mother's Name: Boyd, Pearl

Ross, Margarite: Female, Born: August 16, 1919, Father's Name: Ross, David — Mother's Name: Graves, Jenny

PAGE 164:

Ross, Evelyne Wenonal: Female, Born: November 8, 1920, Father's Name: Ross, David — Mother's Name: Graves, Jennie

PAGE 176:

Sceaver, Pearlie May: Female, Born: June 10, 1918, Father's Name: Sceaver, Cecil — Mother's Name: Rumley, Julia

PAGE 178:

Smith, Veola: Female, Born: December 29, 1919, Father's Name: Smith, Garland — Mother's Name: Reeves, Oakley

PAGE 180:

Shepard, Arlene Lorraine: Female, Born: February 11, 1921, Father's Name: Shepard, Dana Earl — Mother's Name: Peterson, Elma

Selby, Edith Evelyn: Female, Born: March 20, 1921, Father's Name: Selby, John — Mother's Name: Reeves, Eva Mae

Stillwell, Chester Clay: Male, Born: April 18, 1921, Father's Name: Stillwell, Charles — Mother's Name: Rhinehart, Rebecca

Smith, Catherine: Female, Born: June 11, 1921, Father's Name: Smith, James — Mother's Name: Smith, Isabell

Sapp, Bernice Eliza: Female, Born: June 24, 1921, Father's Name: Sapp, Owen — Mother's Name: Nichols, Ruth Hannah

PAGE 198:
Tate, Roy August: Male, Born: November 19, 1918, Father's Name: Tate, Joseph — Mother's Name: Gibson, Lydia

Froselius, Marion Louise: No gender given, Born: December 11, 1918, Father's Name: Froselius, Hugo Emanuel — Mother's Name: Akers, Inez Elizabeth

Thomas, Constance Bessie: Female, Born: July 9, 1919, Father's Name: Thomas, H.W. — Mother's Name: Humphey, Bessie

PAGE 212:
Vargarko, Unnamed: Male, Born: November 25, 1918, Father's Name: Vargarko, Andy — Mother's Name: Vasko, Mary

PAGE 214:
Walker, Madeline Beryl: Female, Born: April 16, 1918, Father's Name: Walker, Ole P. — Mother's Name: Cox, Merle

Weadlee, Garnett Ruth: Female, Born: May 14, 1918, Father's Name: Weadlee, W.H. — Mother's Name: Felton, Leila

PAGE 216:
Williams, Paris Theoplas: No gender given, Born: March 1, 1921, Father's Name: Williams, Paris — Mother's Name: William Bessie

West, Alice: Female, Born: December 24, 1920, Father's Name: West, Leonard — Mother's Name: West, Margaret

West, Alta: Female, Born: December 24, 1920, Father's Name: West, Leonard — Mother's Name: West, Margaret

A display cabinet from the Monroe Mercantile Company (the Buxton company store run by Consolidated Coal), on display in the Monroe County Historical Society museum.

Monroe County Iowa Delayed Birth Records

Early in the 20th century many births took place at home, and registering births was not required by law. Though sometimes doctors and midwives took care of filing the pertinent information, some births were not registered until long afterwards – sometimes only when the person filed to collect Social Security or another type of pension and had to prove age and status.

This section of the book lists births taking place in Buxton which were not reported and documented until later.

Information Recorded:
This book contains: Child's Name, Race, Gender, Birth Date, Father's Place of Birth, Father's Age, Father's Name, Mother's Place of Birth, Mother's Age, Mother's Maiden Name, Date of Filing.

PAGE 240:
Bloom, Anna Karen: White, Female, Born: November 21, 1895, Father: Bloom, Carl, No age given, Born: Sweden, Mother: Peterson, Ida C., No age given, Born: Sweden, Date filed: September 24, 1941

Bloom, Arthur Robert: White, Male, Born: October 23, 1891, Father: Bloom, Carl, No age given, Born: Sweden, Mother: Peterson, Ida C., No age given, Born: Sweden, Date filed: September 24, 1941

PAGE 244:
Anderson, Carl Arthur: White, Male, Born: August 19, 1904, Father: Anderson, Frank Edmon, No age given, Born: Sweden, Mother: Carlson, Ida Augusta, No age given, Born: Illinois, Date filed: March 23, 1942

PAGE 247:
Johnson, Leon Arthur: White, Male, Born: October 6, 1922, Father: Johnson, Ludwig, No age given, Born: Sweden, Mother: Carlson, Sigrid, No age given, Born: Jackson Co., Minnesota, Date filed: March 23, 1942

PAGE 248:

Smith, Early William: White, Male, Born: August 30, 1911, Father: Smith, William B., No age given, Born: Iowa, Mother: Vaugh, Anna, No age given, Born: Iowa, Date filed: April 18, 1942

PAGE 249:

Isaacson, Madie Louise: White, Female, Born: October 16, 1912, Father: Isaacson, Charles, No age given, Born: Stockholm, Sweden, Mother: Fisher, Mary Ann, No age given, Born: Streater, Illinois, Date filed: April 29, 1942

PAGE 250:

Farley, Maybelle: Black, Female, Born: January 26, 1914, Father: Farley, Elder, No age given, Born: Louisiana, Mother: Roach, Maggie, No age given, Born: Thurber, Texas, Date filed: May 4, 1942

Chester, Myrle Walter: White, Male, Born: March 3, 1912, Father: Chester, Clarence, No age given, Born: Mahaska Co., Iowa, Mother: Claver, Lillie, No age given, Born: Monroe Co., Iowa, Date filed: May 4, 1942

Lee, William Washington: Black, Male, Born: January 23, 1910, Father: Lee, William Washington Sr., No age given, Born: Virginia, Mother: Pugh, Alberta, No age given, Born: Leon, Iowa, Date filed: May 5, 1942

PAGE 255:

Mays, Leonard William: Black, Male, Born: August 6, 1918, Father: Mays, Leonard Wm., No age given, Born: Virginia, Mother: Washington, Anna, No age given, Born: Iowa, Date filed: June 3, 1942

PAGE 258:

Onder, Thomas: White, Male, Born: September 6, 1920, Father: Onder, John, No age given, Born: Czechoslovakia, Mother: Kocera, Barbara, No age given, Born: Czechoslovakia, Date filed: June 11, 1942

PAGE 261:

Smith, Clarence Richard: White, Male, Born: June 16, 1922, Father: Smith, Wm. B., No age given, Born: Chariton, Iowa, Mother: Vaughn, Anna, No age given, Born: Muchakinock, Mahaska Co, Iowa, Date filed: July 3, 1942

PAGE 262:

Schoolen, Mary Rosalie: White, Female, Born: February 6, 1914, Father: Schoolen, John, No age given, Born: Oskaloosa, Iowa, Mother: Hughbanks, Belle, No age given, Born: Eddyville, Iowa, Date filed: July 6, 1914

Pratt, Phillip Dale: White, Male, Born: February 6, 1914, Father: Pratt, Stewart M., No age given, Born: Muscatine Co., Iowa, Mother: Neighbor, Isabel, No age given, Born: Hiteman, Monroe Co, Iowa, Date filed: July 9, 1942

PAGE 265:

Allison, Alfred Wesley: White, Male, Born: July 16, 1891, Father: Allison, George, No age given, Born: Pennsylvania, Mother: Parker, Emma, No age given, Born: Missouri, Date filed: July 27, 1942

PAGE 270:

Kietzman, Arthur Alex: White, Male, Born: January 24, 1913, Father: Kietzman, Robert William, No age given, Born: Germany, Mother: Boze, Millie, No age given, Born: Geneseo, Illinois, Date Filed: August 22, 1942

PAGE 271:

Atkinson, Milton: Black, Male, Born: November 15, 1893, Father: Atkinson, Sam, No age given, Born: Virginia, Mother: Blakenson, Mary, No age given, Born: Virginia, Date filed: August 26, 1942

West, Leonard Andrew: Black, Male, Born: October 24, 1921, Father: West, Lenard A., Age 26, Born: Guthrie, Kentucky, Mother: Payne, Margaret Victor, Age 19, Born: Toluca, Illinois, Date filed: August 27, 1942

PAGE 274:

Griffin, Lucy Marie: White, Female, Born: February 26, 1905, Father: Griffin, Walter, Age 22, Born: Monroe Co., Iowa, Mother: Vaughn, Anna, Age 18, Born: Mahaska Co., Iowa, Date filed: September 8, 1942

Smith, Emma Alvena: White, Female, Born: May 15, 1916, Father: Smith, Wm. B., Age 40, Born: Lucas Co., Iowa, Mother: Vaugh, Anna, Age 29, Born: Mahaska Co., Iowa, Date filed: September 8, 1942

Smith, Georgia Mae: White, Female, Born, November 19, 1907, Father: Smith, Wm. B., Age 32, Born: Lucas Co., Iowa, Mother: Vaughn, Anna, Age 21, Born: Mahaska Co, Iowa, Date filed: September 8, 1942

Thomas, Claver Ann: White, Female, Born: December 15, 1907, Father: Thomas, David L., Age 24, Born: Beacon, Mahaska Co., Iowa, Mother: Nickell, Leah Dell, Age 22, Born: Springfield, Nebraska, Date filed: September 9, 1942

PAGE 275:

Slofkaski, Anna Agnes: White, Female, Born: November 1, 1919, Father: Slofkaski, Mike, Age 42, Born: Austria, Mother: Ferkas, Polly, Age 32, Born: Austria, Date filed: September 10, 1942

Olson, Roy Henry: White, Male, Born: April 12, 1918, Father: Olson, Richard, Age 44, Born: Sweden, Mother: Nylander, Tekla Josephine, Age 37, Born: Sweden, Date filed: September 10, 1942

Law, Betty Louise: White, Female, Born: June 10, 1921, Father: Law, Earl Elmer, Age 33, Born: Washington, Mother: Anderson, Vendla M., Age 32, Born: Mahaska Co., Iowa, Date filed: September 14, 1942

Law, Marvin Elmo: White, Male, Born: November 18, 1918, Father: Law, Earl Elmer, Age 30, Born: Washington, Mother: Anderson, Vendla M., Age 29, Born: Mahaska Co., Iowa, Date filed: September 14, 1942

PAGE 276:

Antolik, John Harold: White, Male, Born: August 13, 1913, Father: Antolik, Stephan J., Age 31, Born: Austria, Mother: Chanko, Elizabeth, Age 35, Born: Austria, Date filed: September 19, 1942

PAGE 278:

Rumley, Mary Odessa: Black, Female, Born: May 16, 1921, Father: Rumley, General H., Age 48, Born: Virginia, Mother: Boyd, Pearl Mable, Age 38, Born: Kansas, Date filed: September 26, 1942

PAGE 279:

McBride, Everett Vern: White, Male, Born: July 30, 1904, Father: McBride, Francis Benjamin, Age 47, Born: Tennessee, Mother: Scott, Laura Bell, Age 44, Born: Not given, Date filed: September 28, 1942

PAGE 280:

Antolik, John Harold: White, Male, Born: August 13, 1913, Father: Antolik, Stephan J., Age 31, Born: Austria, Mother: Chunko, Elizabeth, Age 35, Born: Austria, Date filed: October 1, 1942

PAGE 281:

Lenger, Christiana: White, Female, Born: October 7, 1906, Father: Lenger, Michael, Age 25, Born: Czechoslovakia, Mother: Haydeck, Anna, Age 24, Born: Pennsylvania, Date filed: October 3, 1942

PAGE 283:

Connell, Nellie Marie Catherine: White, Female, Born: February 13, 1906, Father: Connell, Robert, Age 28, Born: Scotland, Mother: McPherson, Julie, Age 27, Born: Fernwick, Scotland, Date filed: October 16, 1942

Craggett, Ethel Hortense: Black, Female, Born: October 11, 1903, Father: Craggett, James Patterson, Age 24, Born: Virginia, Mother: Wright, Molly, Age 20, Born: Virginia, Date filed: October 19, 1942

Lewis, Thomas Timothy Jr.: Black, Male, Born: October 28, 1916, Father: Lewis, Thomas T., Age 27, Born: Iowa, Mother: Strother, Mabel Elizabeth, Age 27, Born: Washington, Date filed: October 21, 1942

PAGE 284:

Austin, Chester Lawrence: White, Male, Born: October 9, 1909, Father: Austin, Harry C., Age 28, Born: South Dakota, Mother: Lawrence, Blanche Carolyn, Age 28, Born: Iowa, Date filed: October 22, 1942

PAGE 285:

Benson, Hazel Harriet: White, Female, Born: February 23, 1916, Father: Benson, Thomas Jefferson, Age 28, Born: Iowa, Mother: Brantingham, Gladys Pauline, Age 26, Born: Iowa, Date filed: October 29, 1942

PAGE 286:

Smith, Nellie Elizabeth: White, Female, Born: May 14, 1911, Father: Smith, James Franklin, Age 40, Born: Putnam Co., North Virginia, Mother: Rice, Sarah Elizabeth, Age 45, Born: Arnton Co., Ohio, Date filed: October 30, 1942

Buxton Wonders baseball team. The fourth man from the left in the back row is identified as John Pritchard Burkett.

Gray, Lois Leonard: White, Male, Born: July 20, 1919, Father: Gray, Robert Herbert, Age 43, Born: Kentucky, Mother: Bradbury, Lily May, Age 40, Born: Kansas, Date filed: November 2, 1942

Doyle, Rosa Mae: Black, Female, Born: June 10, 1910, Father: Doyle, Peter, Age 41, Born: Virginia, Mother: Carr, Mary Belle, Age 24, Born: Lynchburg, Virginia, Date filed: November 3, 1942

PAGE 288:

James, Alphonso: Black, Male, Born: March 28, 1909, Father: James, R.H., Age 33, Born: West Virginia, Mother: Oiland, Martha, Age 28, Missouri, , Date filed: November 13, 1942

Peterson, Wilma Louise: White, Female, Born: March 27, 1916, Father: Peterson, David Alexius, Age 32, Born: Sweden, Mother: Nylander, Emma Louise, Age 29, Born: Sweden, Date filed: November 16, 1942

Beaman, Alberta: Black, Female, Born: December 15, 1917, Father: Beaman, Archie, Age 44, Born: Alabama, Mother: Boyd, Julia, Age 38, Born: Missouri, Date filed: November 17, 1942

PAGE 289:

Peterson, Linnea Dorothy: White, Female, Born: February 27, 1913, Father: Peterson, David Alexius, Age 29, Born: Sweden, Mother: Nylander, Emma Louise, Age 26, Born: Mahaska Co., Iowa, Date filed: November 20, 1942

PAGE 291:

Playton, Mary: White, Female, Born: November 21, 1910, Father: Playton, John, Age 34, Born: Lithuania, Mother: Jancious, Mary, Age 29, Born: Lithuania, Date filed: December 1, 1942

PAGE 292:

Reiplinger, Edward John: White, Male, Born: September 13, 1908, Father: Reiplinger, Frank James, Age 28, Born: Illinois, Mother: Bradley, Violet, Age 28, Born: Quebec, Canada, Date filed: December 5, 1942

PAGE 294:

Johnson, Louise Odessa: White, Female, Born: January 26, 1916, Father: Johnson, George Dallas, Age 49, Born: Iowa, Mother: Foglesong,, Lucy, Age 35, Born: Iowa, Date filed: December 26, 1942

PAGE 297:

Holland, Edith M.: Black, Female, Born: January 9, 1911, Father: Holland, John, Age 38, Born: Virginia, Mother: Tansel, Sarah, Age 39, Born: Alabama, Date filed: January 16, 1943

PAGE 299:
Isaacson, Eric Chester: White, Male, Born: October 7, 1921, Father: Isaacson, Joseph Chas., Age 22, Born: Iowa, Mother: Pierce, Thelma Jenevieve, Age 19, Born: Iowa, Date filed: January 30, 1943

PAGE 302:
Mays, Gertrude Yvonne: Black, Female, Born: October 12, 1915, Father: Mays, James Wesley, Age 24, Born: Staunton, Virginia, Mother: Kennedy, Pearl Ermeta, Age 21, Born: Ottumwa, Iowa, Date filed: February 13, 1943

PAGE 304:
Neely, Ethel Jane: Black, Female, Born: April 28, 1913, Father: Neely, John Woodford, Age 44, Born: Frankfort, Kentucky, Mother: Tibbs, Lena, Age 42, Born: Danville, Kentucky, Date filed: February 25, 1943

Lafayette, Gladys Mantelle: Black, Female, Born: December 26, 1904, Father: LaFayette, Jesse, Age 28, Born: Iowa, Mother: Gant, Christina Geneva, Age 22, Born: Iowa, Date filed: February 26, 1943

PAGE 307:
Merrill, Willard C.: White, Male, Born: March 14, 1916, Father: Merrill, Charles A., Age 32, Born: Monroe Co., Iowa, Mother: Fry, Martha Hellen, Age 29, Born: Monroe Co., Iowa, Date filed: March 9, 1943

PAGE 308:
Wilson, Juanita: Black, Female, Born: September 22, 1911, Father: Wilson, Luke, Age 40, Born: North Carolina, Mother: Rolls, Dora, Age 30, Born: Missouri, Date filed: March 13, 1943

PAGE 311:
Cerovac, Antoinette: White, Female, Born: January 16, 1913, Father: Cerovac, Frank, Age 38, Born: Yugoslavia, Mother: Cerovac, Antonia, Date filed: March 31, 1943

Pierce, Marjorie Mary: White, Female, Born: July 15, 1918, Father: Pierce, Elmer Leon, Age 20, Born: Monroe Co., Iowa, Mother: Binah, Dorotha Hickman, Age 18, Born: Lucas Co., Iowa, Date filed: April 5, 1943

PAGE 314:

Lewis, Mabel: Black, Female, Born: May 21, 1920, Father: Lewis, Thomas Timothy, Sr., Age 29, Born: Mahaska Co., Iowa, Mother: Strother, Mabel Elizabeth, Age 30, Born: Washington, D.C., Date Filed: May 1, 1943

PAGE 318:

Turner, Gilbert Lloyd: Black, Male, Born: July 7, 1910, Father: Turner, Will Lucius, Age 23, Born: Tennessee, Mother: Jones, Bessie Bell, Age 22, Born: Iowa, Date filed: June 1, 1943

PAGE 319:

Nalevanko, Elizabeth L.: White, Female, Born: December 28, 1908, Father: Nalevanko, Andrew, Age not given, Born: Austria, Mother: Kapinus, Age 22, Born: Austria, Date filed: June 7, 1943

Lash, Carmaletta: White, Female, Born: April 10, 1919, Illegitimate, Father: No information given, Mother: Lash, Nellie, Age 17, Born: Missouri, Date filed: June 14, 1943

PAGE 323:

Argenta, Jessie Mary: White, Female, Born: June 29, 1924, Father: Argenta, Virgil, Age 20, Born: Arten, Italy, Mother: Zanoni, Thressa Shara, Age 19, Born: Arten, Italy, Date filed: July 31, 1943

Mays, Jacqueline: Black, Female, Born: July 6, 1922, Father: Mays, Leonard, Age 26, Born: Staunton, Virginia, Mother: Washington, Anna May, Age 26, Born: Staunton, Virginia, Date filed: August 9, 1943

PAGE 324:

Reiplinger, Kathleen: White, Female, Born: July 4, 1909, Father: Reiplinger, Frank Henry, Age 29, Born: Chicago, Illinois, Mother: Bradley, Violet, Age 29, Born: Quebec, Canada, Date filed: September 9, 1943

PAGE 326:

Burton, Corine: Black, Female, Born: March 2, 1921, Father: Burton, Henry Clay, Age 23, Born: Alabama, Mother: Taylor, Oleava, Age 16, Born: Missouri, Date filed: September 14, 1943

PAGE 327:

Gross, Mildred Cora: White, Female, Born: October 4, 1912, Father: Gross, William, Age 34, Born: Czechoslovakia, Mother: Spurney, Catherine, Age 34, Born: Czechoslovakia, Date filed: September 25, 1943

Mays, Thelma Rosella: Black, Female, Born: January 1, 1915, Father: Mays, Leonard, Age 20, Born: Virginia, Mother: Washington, Anna Mae, Age 20, Born: Virginia, Date filed: September 17, 1943

PAGE 332:

Rustan, Gyle Alfred: White, Male, Born: October 27, 1913, Father: Rustan, Albin Gust, Age 31, Born: Iowa, Mother: Richmond, Nellie Ethel, Age 21, Born: Iowa, Date filed: November 9, 1943

Johnson, Linnea Josephine: White, Female, Born: March 11, 1905, Father: Johnson, Carl John, Age 27, Born: Sweden, Mother: Flodman, Tekla Josephine, Age 32, Born: Sweden, Date filed: November 15, 1943

PAGE 334:

Gustofson, Frank E.: White, Male, Born: July 15, 1913, Father: Gustofson, Frank, Age 40, Born: Sweden, Mother: Elison, Hanna, Age not given, Born: Sweden, Date filed: December 24, 1943

PAGE 337:

Dish, Violet J.: White, Female, Born: July 12, 1921, Father: Dish, Joseph, Age 29, Born: Panevezia, Russia, Mother: Pugacauskaite, Marcella, Age 21, Born: Vilna, Russia, Date filed: February 5, 1944

PAGE 340:

Carson, Hugh Fowler: White, Male, Born: November 16, 1903, Father: Carson, Embert, Age 29, Born: Pella, Iowa, Mother: Fowler, Alice Jeanette, Age 35, Born: Abbington, Illinois, Date filed: April 4, 1944

Corum, Clara: White, Female, Born: March 20, 1915, Father: Corum, William, Age 29, Born: Iowa, Mother: Gordon, Bertha, Age 27, Born: Missouri, Date filed: April 4, 1944

PAGE 342:

Engstrom, Violet: White, Female, Born: May 26, 1913, Father: Engstrom, Gust, Age 45, Born: Sweden, Mother: Larson, Rena, Age 38, Born: Sweden, Date filed: May 13, 1944

PAGE 343:

Sickle, Ann: White, Female, Born: December 15, 1926, Father: Sickle, John, Age 31, Born: Pennsylvania, Mother: Klobnak, Mary, Age 29, Born: Czechoslovakia, Date filed: May 13, 1944

PAGE 344:

Gillette, Robert E.: Black, Male, Born: January 27, 1912, Father: Gillette, William Lewis, Age 42, Born: Virginia, Mother: Carter, Carrie, Age 34, Born: Virginia, Date filed: June 12, 1944

Johnson, Nadine Lavaugh: White, Female, Born: March 14, 1919, Father: Johnson, George Dallas, Age not given, Born: Iowa, Mother: Foglesong, Lucy Sherlock, Age 38, Born: Iowa, Date filed: June 19, 1944

PAGE 346:

Winkler, John Henry: White, Male, Born: May 29, 1923, Father: Winkler, Thomas, Age 26, Born: Austria, Mother: Krapple, Helen, Age 26, Born: Austria, Date filed: July 19, 1944

PAGE 348:

Turner, Robert David: Black, Male, Born: October 19, 1907, Father: Turner, Will Lucius, Age not given, Born: Tennessee, Mother: Jones, Bessie, Age 20, Born: Iowa, Date filed: September 5, 1944

PAGE 349:

Lacy, Albert J.: White, Male, Born: September 16, 1915, Father: Lacy, John S., Age 23, Born: Austria, Mother: Martis, Susie, Age 19, Born: Central City, Illinois, Date filed: October 16, 1944

PAGE 351:

Wise, Laura Ethel: White, Female, Born: February 19, 1916, Father: Wise, Emmett Ward, Age 39, Born: Missouri, Mother: Downey, Florence, Age 31, Born: Iowa, Date filed: January 17, 1945

PAGE 358:

Wilson, Mae: White, Female, Born: August 15, 1904, Father: Wilson, Frank Martin, Age 23, Born: Iowa, Mother: Downey, Florence, Age 20, Born: Missouri, Date filed: July 3, 1945

PAGE 359:

Kolesor, Andrew: White, Male, Born: August 12, 1912, Father: Kolesor, George, Age not given, Born: Czechoslovakia, Mother: Gallo, Anna, Age not given, Born: Czechoslovakia, Date filed: September 1, 1945

PAGE 363:

Gedda, Charles: White, Male, Born: April 7, 1912, Father: Gedda, Anthony, Age not given, Born: Italy, Mother: Coram, Mary, Age not given, Born: Missouri, Date filed: August 22, 1946

PAGE 369:

Lee, William Gerald: White, Male, Born: October 6, 1913, Father: Lee, William John, Age not given, Born: Wales, Mother: Coop, Betsy Stewart, Age not given, Born: Iowa, Date filed: March 22, 1948

PAGE 371:

Garland, William E.: Black, Male, Born: September 23, 1915, Father: Garland, George, Age not given, Born: Iowa, Mother: Brooks, Frances, Age not given, Born: West Virginia, Date filed: October 1, 1948

PAGE 372:

Demichelis, William: White, Male, Born: October 6, 1914, Father: Demichelis, John Baptist, Age not given, Born: Italy, Mother: Matouda, Madeline, Age not given, Born: Italy, Date filed: January 3, 1949

PAGE 374:

Schoolen, Paul Edgar: White, Male, Born: February 27, 1920, Father: Schoolen, Patrick, Age not given, Born: Iowa, Mother: Bringman, Blanche, Age not given, Born: Iowa, Date filed: June 13, 1949

PAGE 375:

Gaines, Donald: Black, Male, Born: December 12, 1917, Father: Gaines, Reuben, Age not given, Born: Virginia, Mother: Strother, Bertha, Age not given, Born: Virginia, Date filed: September 28, 1949

PAGE 378:

Maughan, Ethel May: White, Female, Born: September 13, 1898, Father: Maughan, John Joseph, Age not given, Born: England, Mother: Thompson, Jane Ann, Age not given, Born: England, Date filed: December 21, 1950

PAGE 380:

Hall, Henry Mardew: White, Male, Born: August 27, 1911, Father: Hall, William, Age not given, Born: Scotland, Mother: Williamson, Anna, Age not given, Born: Scotland, Date filed: December 21, 1950

PAGE 382:

Heitz, William Franklin: White, Male, Born: March 8, 1920, Father: Heitz, William Tomas, Age not given, Born: Rushville, Illinois, Mother: Helmick, Lula, Age not given, Born: Tracey, Iowa, Date filed: June 1, 1951

Wilcox, Richard Douglas: White, Male, Born: August 9, 1916, Father: Wilcox, Charles Chester, Age not given, Born: Iowa, Mother: Lesen, Lillie B., Age not given, Born: Iowa, Date filed: August 4, 1951

PAGE 384:

Franklin, Natalie: Black, Female, Born: February 19, 1908, Father: Franklin, Harry Kenneth, Age not given, Born: Iowa, Mother: Green, Anna Louise, Age not given, Born: Iowa, Date filed: December 1, 1951

Lacy, Anna Marie: White, Female, Born: May 3, 1915, Father: Lacy, Andrew, Age not given, Born: Czechoslovakia, Mother: Krupar, Elizabeth, Age not given, Born: Czechoslovakia, Date filed: December 1, 1951

PAGE 385:

Fleming, Harold Dean: White Male, Born: April 16, 1912, Father: No information given, Mother: Long, Anna, Age not given, Born: Iowa, Date filed: April 11, 1952

Olson, Emma Josephine: White, Female, Born: March 5, 1911, Father: Olson, R.O., Age not given, Born: Sweden, Mother: Nylander, Tekla, Age not given, Born: Sweden, Date filed: April 14, 1952

PAGE 386:

Burkett, Oliver: Black, Male, Born: April 26, 1917, Father: Burkett, Henry Phillip, Age not given, Born: Charlottesville, Virginia, Mother: Wheeler, Mary Elizabeth, Age not given, Born: Metropolis, Illinois, Date filed: April 30, 1952

PAGE 389:

Cadell, Alice Irene: White, Female, Born: February 26, 1913, Father: Cadell, Gus, Age not given, Born: Iowa, Mother: Anderson, Gertrude, Age not given, Born: Iowa, Date filed: March 30, 1953

PAGE 394:

Reasby, Anthony Swan: Black, Male, Born: September 10, 1903, Father: Reasby, Lewis, Age not given, Born: Virginia, Mother: Austin, Rena, Age not given, Born: Alabama, Date filed: March 19, 1954

PAGE 400:

Smith, Lonnie Harold: Black, Male, Born: July 11, 1911, Father: Smith, Daniel, Age not given, Born: Virginia, Mother: Martin, Amy Lee, Age not given, Born: Virginia, Date filed: May 31, 1955

PAGE 403:

Zaring, June Patricia: White, Female, Born: February 22, 1920, Father: Zaring, John Leroy, Age not given, Born: Iowa, Mother: Bates, Mary Ann, Age not given, Born: Iowa, Date filed: December 16, 1955

PAGE 404:

Weir, John Edgar: White, Male, Born: September 9, 1903, Father: Weir, Robert, Age not given, Born: Streeter, Illinois, Mother: Peterson, Elizabeth, Age not given, Born: Bartensville, Illinois, Date filed: February 21, 1956

PAGE 406:

Miles, Frances Aleatha: Black, Female, Born: May 11, 1923, Father: Miles, Cliford, Age not given, Born: Muchakinock, Iowa, Mother: Clayborne, Estella, Age not given, Born: Enterprise, Iowa, Date filed: June 6, 1956

PAGE 416:

Peterson, Viola Elizabeth: White, Female, Born: May 29, 1913, Father: Peterson, Olaf N., Age not given, Born: Sweden, Mother: Bergquist, Hannah, Age not given, Born: Iowa, Date filed: March 24, 1959

PAGE 417:

Peterson, Bernice: White, Female, Born: May 13, 1910, Father: Peterson, Olaf N. Age not given, Born: Sweden, Mother: Bergquist, Hannah, Age not given, Born: Iowa, Date filed: May 2, 1959

PAGE 418:

Nevins, Freda Bernice: White, Female, Born: February 3, 1903, Father: Nevins, Charles Wesley, Age not given, Born: Indiana, Mother: Johnson, Lula Armeta, Age not given, Born: Wapello Co., Iowa, Date filed: September 30, 1959

Olson, John Albert: White, Male, Born: April 20, 1904, Father: Olson, John B., Age not given, Born: Sweden, Mother: Larson, Anna Sofie, Age not given, Born: Sweden, Date filed: October 22, 1959

PAGE 419:

Peterson, Anna Lynette: White, Female, Born: December 4, 1911, Father: Peterson, Olaf N., Age not given, Born: Sweden, Mother: Bergquist, Hannah, Age not given, Born: Iowa, Date filed: March 8, 1960

PAGE 421:

Kennedy, Edith Mae: White, Female, Born: February 15, 1908, Father: Kennedy, William Harve, Age not given, Born: Illinois, Mother: Daugherty, Mary, Age not given, Born: Not given, Date filed: November 1, 1960

PAGE 423:

Bryant, John Wilbert: Black, Male, Born: January 22, 1912, Father: Bryant, Orville, Age not given, Born: Iowa, Mother: Walker, Hazel, Age not given, Born: Iowa, Date filed: February 20, 1962

PAGE 424:

Lee, David Morgan Jr.: White, Male, Born: January 10, 1919, Father: Lee, David, Age not given, Born: Keokuk Co., Iowa, Mother: Turner, Sarah, Age not given, Born: Illinois, Date filed: August 15, 1962

PAGE 427:

Melchiaric, Peter E.: White, Male, Born: October 26, 1912, Father: Melchiaric, Andrew, Age not given, Born: Italy, Mother: Waters, Georgia May, Age not given, Born: Iowa, Date filed: September 11, 1964

Onder, Albert: White, Male, Born: December 26, 1924, Father: Onder, John, Age not given, Born: Czechoslovakia, Mother: Kocera, Barbara, Age not given, Born: Czechoslovakia, Date filed: December 14, 1964

PAGE 429:

Frazen, Harold Navo: White, Male, Born: May 25, 1915, Father: Frazen, John, Age not given, Born: Missouri, Mother: McCanna, Maggie, Age not given, Born: Iowa, Date filed: December 13, 1966

Frazen, Marvin Morgan: White, Male, Born: August 7, 1912, Father: Frazen, John, Age not given, Born: Missouri, Mother: McCanna, Maggie, Age not given, Born: Iowa, Date filed: December 13, 1966

Onder, Mary Margery: White, Female, Born: September 27, 1922, Father: Onder, John, Age not given, Born: Czechoslovakia, Mother: Kocera, Barbara, Age not given, Born: Czechoslovakia, Date filed: February 14, 1967

PAGE 431:

Lee, Mary Ellen: White, Female, Born: June 10, 1921, Father: Lee, William John, Age not given, Born: Wales, Mother: Coop, Betsy, Age not given, Born: What Cheer, Iowa, Date filed: September 7, 1968

PAGE 432:

Hagglund, Bernice Elizabeth: White, Female, Born: November 26, 1916, Father: Hagglund, Carl Albert, Age not given, Born: Mahaska Co., Iowa, Mother: Blomgren, Elizabeth, Age not given, Born: Mahaska Co., Iowa, Date filed: April 13, 1971

PAGE 433:

Frazen, Maye Marie: White, Female, Born: May 1, 1920, Father: Frazen, John, Age not given, Born: Eddyville, Iowa, Mother: McCannon, Maggie, Age not given, Born: Oskaloosa, Iowa, Date filed: July 29, 1976

Peterson, Charlotte Beatrice: White, Female, Born: April 26, 1916, Father: Peterson, Edward Eugene, Age not given, Born: Not given, Mother: Berquist, Eva Charlotte, Age not given, Born: Not given, Date filed: September 22, 1978

Unidentified Buxton resident. Relatively high wages and household income allowed residents to celebrate special events with professional photographs.

Scroggins, Simeon LaVerne: Black, Male, Born: September 17, 1918, Father: Scroggins, Charles Edward, Age not given, Born: Carrollton, Missouri, Mother: Anderson, Anna Bertha May, Age not given, Born: Carrollton, Missouri, Date filed: October 30, 1978

PAGE 434:

Franzen, Sylvia Jessie: White, Female, Born: March 30, 1920, Father: Franzen, Frank Chester, Age not given, Born: Oskaloosa, Iowa, Mother: Heck, Doris Bertha, Age not given, Born: Pekay, Iowa, Date filed: April 6, 1979

PAGE 435:

Claybourne, Earl: Black, Male, Born: February 9, 1919, Father: Claybourne, Alford, Age not given, Born: Wapello Co., Iowa, Mother: Nichols, Allie, Age not given, Born: Polk Co., Iowa, Date filed: July 1, 1980

Hawkins, John: Black, Male, Born: July 6, 1921, Father: Hawkins, Henry C., Age not given, Born: Virginia, Mother: Vincent, Isabell, Age not given, Born: Iowa, Date filed: August 25, 1980

Frazier, Winfield Harlan: White, Male, Born: March 13, 1920, Father: Frazier, Charles Wesley, Age not given, Born: Monroe Co., Iowa, Mother: Marlowe, Iva Mae, Age not given, Born: Jefferson Co., Iowa, Date filed: July 13, 1981

PAGE 436:

Swanson, Claudine Sara: White, Female, Born: September 6, 1919, Father: Swanson, Swan Levin, Age not given, Born: Pennsylvania, Mother: Hunt, Nora Perleta, Age not given, Born: Colorado, Date filed: September 4, 1981

Dyke, Frances Elizabeth: White, Female, Born: April 7, 1922, Father: Dyke, Aaron, Age not given, Born: Holland, Mother: Prever, Ruby May, Age not given, Born: Drakesville, Iowa, Date filed: August 24, 1982

Jewett, Geraldine: Black, Female, Born: January 26, 1920, Father: Jewett, William, Age not given, Born: Iowa, Mother: Ampey, Margaret, Age not given, Born: Iowa, Date filed: October 27, 1982

PAGE 437:

Pierce, Gladys Darlene: White, Female, Born: October 7, 1919, Father: Pierce, Earl Thurman, Age not given, Born: Iowa, Mother: Humphrey, Ida B., Age not given, Born: Iowa, Date filed: April 9, 1984

[Unknown], Bessie Juanita: Black, Female, Born: December 25, 1922, Father: Williams, Paris, Age not given, Born: Iowa, Mother: Thomas, Bessie, Age not given, No birth place given, Date filed: August 14, 1985
(The last name of this child is listed as Rhodes, but it does not match birth parents names on record)

Carpenter, Annette Kellerman: Black, Female, Born: March 22, 1920, Father: Carpenter, Archie, No age given, Born: West Virginia, Mother: Junkins, Mabel C., Age not given, Born: Bloomfield, Iowa, Date filed: August 29, 1985

PAGE 438:

Williams, Amie Jacqulyn: Black, Female, Born: January 5, 1926, Father: Williams, Paris, Age not given, Born: Virginia, Mother: Williams, Bessie, Age not given, Born: Not given, Date filed: March 5, 1986

Anderson, Dorothy Mae: Black, Female, Born: May 22, 1921, Father: Anderson, William, Age not given, Born: Virginia, Mother: Faidley, Lillie, Age not given, Born: Maryland, Date filed: May 20, 1986

PAGE 439:

Larson, Arvid Lennart: White, Male, Born: December 30, 1909, Father: Larson, Axel Linus, Age not given, Born: Sweden, Mother: Blomgren, Clara Maria, Age not given, Born: Sweden, Date filed: April 4, 1994

Fleck, Howard Eugene: White, Male, Born: December 8, 1911, Father: Fleck, William, Age not given, Born: Iowa, Mother: James, Jennie May, Age not given, Born: Iowa, Date filed: July 9, 1997

PAGE 440:

Green, Doris Lorraine: Black, Female, Born: October 13, 1919, Father: Green, Emery, Age not given, Born: Iowa, Mother: Rhodes, Iva Dolores, Age not given, Born: Iowa, Date filed: October 5, 1998

Buxton Reunion, September 3, 1941. One of the men in the photograph is
Congressman Karl LeCompte (Iowa).

About the Author

Lee Ann Simmers Dickey is a dedicated genealogist who started
researching her own family tree and ended up seeking out records
and documentation for families across the nation. She is also
a proud mother and grandmother. The author of BUXTON ROOTS
as well as BUXTON BRANCHES, she lives in Albia, Iowa.
Her email address is dickeyleeann@yahoo.com.

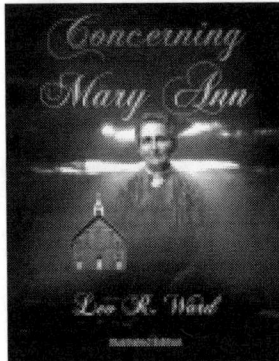

Other books from PBL Limited
publishing and book distribution:

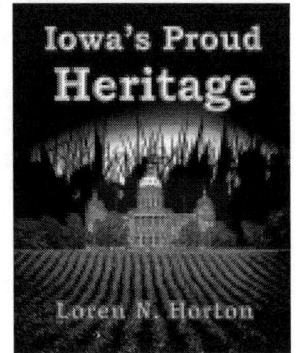

Buxton Roots
Monroe County WPA History
Forever Changed
Concerning Mary Ann
Holding Up the Hills
St. Patrick's Georgetown Iowa
St. Patrick's Legacy
Iowa's Proud Heritage
Coming Up Dry
1904 St. Louis World's Fair

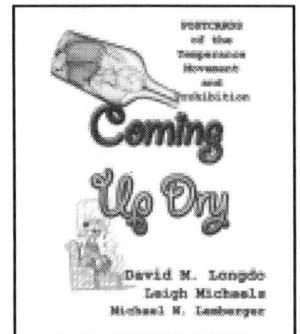

Available at www.pbllimited.com
or at www.Amazon.com
and other online retailers.

Made in the USA
Charleston, SC
17 June 2011